Everyman's Poetry

Everyman, I will go with thee,
and be thy guide

English Sonnets

Selected and edited by A. D. P. BRIGGS

University of Birmingham

EVERYMAN

J. M. Dent · London

This edition first published by Everyman Paperbacks in 1999
Selection, introduction and other critical apparatus
© J. M. Dent 1999

J. M. Dent
Orion Publishing Group
Orion House
5 Upper St Martin's Lane
London WC2H 9EA

Typeset by Deltatype Ltd, Birkenhead, Merseyside
Printed in Great Britain by
The Guernsey Press Co. Ltd, Guernsey C.I.

British Library Cataloguing-in-Publication
Data is available on request.

ISBN 0 460 87990 1

Contents

Note on the Editor

A. D. P. BRIGGS, Professor of Russian Language and Literature at the University of Birmingham, is a specialist in modern Russian Literature, mainly of the nineteenth century, and European poetry. Among his many publications are ten books, five of them devoted to Alexander Pushkin. His editions of Pushkin and FitzGerald's *Omar Khayyam* have already appeared in the Everyman's Poetry series.

Introduction

The sonnet I am not sure about, it seems mechanical.
                                          (Dylan Thomas)

No rapid survey of the sonnet can do justice to such a large and splendid subject. This small poetic instrument can boast of distinguished achievement, high reputation, long life, broad appeal, potent effect and mysterious quality. A foreign import which has been with us now for half a millennium, it has taken over English poetry as no other individual form. Sonnets have been written in thousands, by hundreds of English-speaking poets, including our greatest. Many are facile and mediocre, but the best sonnets, rising to sublime heights of expressiveness, have imprinted themselves indelibly on the nation's poetic memory. Even the coldest hearts of a philistine nation can be stirred by such resonant phrases as these, which come from the sonnets:

> Shall I compare thee to a summer's Day?
>
> If I should die, think only this of me . . .
>
> My name is Ozymandias, king of kings . . .
>
> How do I love thee? Let me count the ways . . .
>
> They also serve who only stand and wait . . .
>
> Death, be not proud . . .

These well-known lines arose in the minds of poets who had undertaken a mechanical task, the writing of a short lyric poem within the limits of a rather strict formula. Fourteen lines, no more, no less, and with systematic rhyming. You might think, with Dylan Thomas, that the exercise is dangerously artificial and scientific, unlikely to produce inspired poetry. But this would be to forget that until recently most of our poetry was written in rhyme, which meant working against the natural grain of language and proceeding from the line-end backwards. All poetry is calculated language; sonnets are most noticeably so. But sonnets have survived from the Middle Ages to the present day, flourishing even in times of avowed spontaneity (the Romantic period) and wild formal experimentation (our own century). Whatever the dangers, sonnets rank among our finest literary treasures. What are the qualities of this form which have made it so attractive and successful?

The word 'sonnet' is a diminutive form of the Latin word '*sonus*' ('a sound') which came to mean 'a little song'. Its deepest origins are probably located in the singing and love poetry of the troubadours, south-European poet-musicians of almost a thousand years ago, but they became crystallised in a recognisable modern form in thirteenth-century Sicily. An early surviving lyric by Piero delle Vigne, 'Natura D'Amore' ('The Nature of Love'), dated around the year 1220, has all the right characteristics of length, metre and rhyme scheme. It is undoubtedly the same kind of sonnet that was brought to perfection more than a century later by the Italian poet, Petrarch.

The Italian (or Petrarchan) sonnet

This is a love-lyric written in iambic pentameter, which means lines with five feet, each of two syllables, with the second one stressed (te-túm, te-túm, te-túm, te-túm, te-túm). Its fourteen lines break down into an eight-line group (*octave*) followed by one of six lines (*sestet*). A strongly established rhyme-scheme gives the poem a clear overall structure. The octave uses only two rhymes: *abba abba*. The sestet has a little more freedom, and may use either two or three rhymes, as in the following possible groups: *cdc cdc, cde cde, cde dce*. The two sections of the poem are normally different in tone. One main idea is deposited in the octave, and it is the task of the sestet to complement or otherwise develop it. For instance, in Petrarch's sonnet 'A Stolen Glove' the poet uses the octave to recollect the beauty of Laura's slender hand, and the sestet to contemplate the (stolen) glove which recently covered it. Petrarch wrote well over 300 such sonnets.

The English (or Shakespearean) sonnet

Another couple of centuries were to pass before the sonnet was imported into England. It came to us through the translations and imitations of first Sir Thomas Wyatt (1503–42) and then Henry Howard, Earl of Surrey (c.1517–47), who decided to change its form. The Italian sonnet can manage with very few rhymes, sometimes only four shared out over the fourteen lines. The English language does not rhyme so easily, and the struggle to find four or more words with the same acoustic ending, accepted by Wyatt, was abandoned by Surrey. His vital innovation was to introduce new rhymes, and alternating ones at that, in the second quatrain, so that *abba abba* became *abab cdcd*. In doing so he was being neither lazy nor unimaginative. He probably foresaw that freedom from excessive tyranny by rhyme could lead to a more natural flow of poetic language and thus to greater spontaneity and sincerity in the expression of the poet's sentiments.

The Italian love sonnet was highly stylised in ideas as well as form, similar conceits being used over and over again. A change in the rhyme scheme of the sonnet in England was the first step towards a new poetic method which would first humanise the expression of love and then make it possible to use the form for other subjects. What was accomplished can be seen by comparing two early sonnets in this book. In Constable's old-style poem, 'Of his Mistress upon Occasion of her Walking in a Garden' (13), the poet uses familiar comparisons; the flowers envy and imitate his mistress's colour and virtue, taking their very sustenance from her beauty and glory. She is divine, life-giving and more flower-like than the flowers themselves. Her eyes are like the sun, responsible for 'living heat'. All of this is said in nice Italianate form (*abba abba cdcdee*). Shakespeare has had enough of this. His mistress's eyes are nothing like the sun, and when she walks she treads upon the ground (23). The warm banality of Shakespeare's poem strikes with wonderful humour against the artificial loftiness of his predecessors. Its naturalness, the deliberate taunt of a confident moderniser, is a direct consequence of the new sonnet form, which sometimes bears Shakespeare's own name since he perfected it in England as Petrarch had done in his country.

The English sonnet still divides into two sections, but the unevenness between them is much increased; twelve lines stand against two. The rhyme scheme is as straightforward as could be imagined: *abab cdcd efef gg*, but the poet now has an even more demanding task. He has to set down an idea in the first quatrain (four lines), develop it in the second and bring it to a kind of culmination in the third, only for that entire group of twelve lines to be subverted, overturned, or else massively endorsed, by the terminal couplet. This not only places a huge burden of responsibility on that couplet, it also presents dangers in the long build-up which comes before. (Successful examples may be seen in 3, 15, 16–25, and 83.) A mediocre poet will simply repeat himself in the second and third quatrains, rather than ensuring that his argument grows steadily and continues to arouse interest. If you want to test a sonneteer for quality, examine the second quatrain of an Italian sonnet or the third quatrain of an English one. These are the places where the poem will lapse into repetitive sogginess if the poet has neglected the proper development of his ideas.

For all its brilliance at the hands of Shakespeare, his sonnet has not been much imitated. Once launched on the mechanical task of sonneteering, poets have preferred to flaunt their ingenuity by taking on the most demanding form, which is Italian. A great majority of the sonnets in this collection are basically Italianate; fine examples may be seen in 79, 102, 139, 170 and 177. Two more are in poems 100 and 127, which is most inappropriate because both of these are dedicated to Shakespeare. John Keats, at least, had the decency to use the English form when writing a sonnet obliquely dedicated to Shakespeare since it was written on a blank page in a collection of his poems (83).

Other sonnet forms

Edmund Spenser (c.1522–99) created a sonnet form which was intended to combine the attractions of the English and Italian. His rhyme scheme, *abab bcbc cdcd ee*, retains the 12 + 2 format but weaves the three quatrains nicely together by picking up one rhyme of the first quatrain for further use in the second and then repeating the process between the second and third. This form, known as the Spenserian sonnet (see 4, 5, 6, 7, 89), never caught on, probably because it retains the difficulty of the Shakespearean one without resolving the problem of finding repeated rhymes.

Spenser returns to the use of only five different rhymes per stanza, where Shakespeare gives himself the liberty of seven.

If Spenser adapted the English sonnet to make it more like the Italian, John Milton (1608–74) attempted almost the reverse. Disliking the sharp break between the octave and the sestet, he decided to ignore it. Several of his sonnets allow the sense to flow strongly across from line 8 to line 9 (enjambement). The required change of tone from the first section of the sonnet to the second is still there, and in roughly the same place, but the turning-point is slightly dislocated from the line-ending, coming a little earlier or later. This is the Miltonic sonnet (34, 35, 45).

The subsequent development of the sonnet was to be more a matter of subject than form, though technical innovations have continued. The last two centuries have seen sonnets combining both basic forms (109), sonnets in couplets (75, 76), a sonnet in reverse (183), a sonnet in monosyllables (189), a sonnet that sneaks in a fifteenth line (112), and several without rhymes, (91) – but no other English poet has a special sonnet to his or her name.

Skewed beauty

The length of the sonnet has something to do with its strong appeal. It is appropriate for the communicating of a good poetic idea, long enough to say something meaningful, short enough to avoid any risk of tedium. Even the (supposed) reduced attention-span of modern times can cope with 115 words at a single draught, which is a rough average of the number of words in an English sonnet. Such a poem is easily readable and memorable, yet substantial enough to contain big thoughts and much beauty. But why not twelve or sixteen? Is there something special about the actual number fourteen? The first thing to be noticed is that it can be divided only by two and seven. The sonnet has no tendency to break down into equal halves, because the unit of seven lines is pretty well unusable in poetry, nor into any other small units *of equal weight*. (Poems of twelve or sixteen lines inevitably sound like quatrain runs.) Fourteen lines have to be broken into smaller sections, and whatever overall pattern you choose, it will be asymmetrical. This is one of the key secrets of the formula.

Let us take this further. Classical sonnets (all sonnets, that is, except a few experimental or modern ones) are written in the most famous line of English poetry, iambic pentameter. This metre is also asymmetrical; it cannot be divided into equal halves. This feature is its greatest glory; our nation's most famous line is characterised by the most delicious sense of imbalance, unpredictability, change and surprise. And so is its most famous stanza. It is the cussed lopsidedness of the sonnet (in two dimensions) which guarantees its renewable originality, freshness and excitement. To drive the point home, we should glance quickly at France, where they like things otherwise. The one great line whose glory the French nation would die for has an extra foot; it is the iambic *hexameter*, otherwise known as the Alexandrine. We scarcely acknowledge the possibility of this line in English poetry; to us it reads like something designed by a committee in Brussels. To make matters worse, French writers have encouraged the obvious tendency for this long line to collapse, exhausted, into two exact halves, by insisting that each line must have a marked break (caesura) in mid-line. The English sonnet tradition has flourished precisely because it has rejected that kind of symmetrical exactitude.

A glance at one sonnet

After so much arid theory about the sonnet it will be useful to bring the genre to life by taking a look at one actual poem. Here is a pleasant specimen from the nineteenth century, 'Letty's Globe' (109), by Charles Tennyson-Turner, the middle brother of the three-poet family, (with its rhyme-scheme marked):

1	When Letty had scarce passed her third glad year,	a
	And her young, artless words began to flow,	b
	One day we gave the child a coloured sphere	a
	Of the wide earth, that she might mark and know,	b
5	By tint and outline, all its sea and land.	c
	She patted all the world; old empires peeped	d
	Between her baby fingers; her soft hand	c
	Was welcome at all frontiers. How she leaped,	d
	And laughed, and prattled in her world-wide bliss;	e
10	But when we turned her sweet unlearned eye	f

On our own isle, she raised a joyous cry,   f
   'Oh! yes, I see it, Letty's home is there!'   g
    And, while she hid all England with a kiss,   e
14 Bright over Europe fell her golden hair.   g

This is a narrative sonnet, telling us a little tale from domestic life concerning a young child. The story develops nicely over the whole poem with no lapses or repetitions. First we learn that the little girl of three or four years has been given a globe so that she can gain a sense of what the world is like. In mid-poem we see what she does with it. She pats it, much amused, and laughs and chatters, enjoying the experience. Her pleasure goes beyond bounds when she is shown where she lives on the surface of the sphere, and she ends in great delight, hugging and kissing the globe. England and Europe are smothered in her childish transports and affection.

Stories should not be too constrained by style, and small children are not easily contained by formality. Therefore the poet has opted for the freest possible exploitation of the sonnet's resources. It is deliberately informal, and difficult to assign to any one sonnet pattern. Starting off like an English sonnet (*abab cdcd*), it ends with a rather weird sestet (*effgeg*), more akin to the Italian. It uses seven rhymes (*à la* Shakespeare) but there is no sharply-rhymed couplet to end with. Thus the poem has no sense of hackneyed form; in its originality it draws on both traditions.

The arrangement of the four main utterances in the poem is interesting. The first one is nicely lopsided, spilling over from the first quatrain into the second and finishing at the end of line 5. The second is shorter, and it ends in mid-line (line 8), not what a poem should do if it wants to end in a proper sestet. The next five lines all run together and end in good Shakespearean fashion at line 12. This gives the effect of a terminal couplet (13–14) – but without any rhymed support. Over all, this poem is nearer than most to the flow of ordinary speech, because it flouts so many of the detailed niceties demanded of a well-behaved sonnet. Kings and queens may require order and elegance; little girls will sprawl all over the place. It is by defying, rather than honouring, canonised patterns of sonnet-structure that this poem achieves its delightful end. The structure of this poem is immaculate in its disorder. Without experience of what sonnets are normally called upon to do, our awareness of this one's quality would be impaired.

Little Letty guides us through a series of experiences, blundering upon moral and political truths which can mean nothing to her, though they speak eloquently to us enchanted adult onlookers. Her first instincts are to pat, love, cherish, hug and kiss. How we regret the erosion of these wonderful impulses in the grown-up world. Her innocence takes her across all frontiers. Her enjoyment of life here and now mocks the passing of entire lost empires. Letty's globe is our earth, and our hold on it is as tenuous and transient as hers. She reminds us of what we are in danger of forgetting: that life is short, power is meaningless, love is all. It is no exaggeration of the sonnet's evocative power to claim that ideas of this magnitude can resonate in the mind even as we watch what seems to be a simple domestic incident. The sonnet works its magic well. Because it is so nicely conceived and constructed its full potential has been realised. Look very closely and you may think there are too many endearing adjectives: young, artless, baby, soft, sweet, joyous, and the like. But who, knowing the overwhelming charm of a three-year-old girl, would consider them gratuitous? The poem would gain nothing by being pruned. A little prattling is in tune with its subject. (This is too early for full-blown Victorian sentimentality.) Most importantly, the poem gains by being wrapped up in the familiar, but not too familiar, vestments of a traditional form. Here is a good example of what the sonnet can do.

Changing the subject

Letty and her globe stand about half way along the line of development in subject matter from mediaeval to modern times. The first sonnets were all about love, then God and death became permissible subjects. Milton opened up further possibilities by writing about his own affliction (34), but it was only at the end of the eighteenth century that the sonnet, reborn after long neglect, was pressed into much broader service. Wordsworth massively extended its scope in writing more than 500 such pieces, not all of them masterpieces. The present collection includes at least one example of a weak sonnet, in his patriotic marking of the Battle of Waterloo (55). Its archaic bombast shows that the composition of poetry sometimes came too easily to this poet, whose inconsistency was amusingly derided by another sonneteer (172). During the nineteenth century the sonnet truly spread its wings and could deal with almost any decent subject, from crocodiles (91) and sea-monsters (103) to separating lovers (108), silence (112), science (114), cheesecake (90) and even nuptial sleep (133). The twentieth century has removed all barriers to subject matter, and the sonnet has wandered into every last area of human experience. It has not been possible to include many recent sonnets in this collection, but an example of how far things have moved since the innocent early days of this form can be seen in the very title of John Updike's caustic sonnet of lost love: 'No More Access to Her Underpants' (190).

Wyatt's modest innovation in the early sixteenth century, improved by Surrey and Sidney and brought to perfection by Shakespeare, has now grown into a literary industry of dynastic proportions. The sonnet has come to love and admire both its larger family and its own ego. It has often peered into its own soul, considering the status, methods and mysteries by which it lives (43, 46, 52, 62, 84, 129). Sonneteer has written to sonneteer (51, 73, 100, 127, 130, 172). One sonnet has re-evoked another by recycling its opening line (9 and 53; 94 and 142; 97 and 185). Wordsworth's famous advice for us not to scorn the sonnet (52) has been followed on a huge scale. This collection ends with a further plea, for us not to scorn 'The sonnet on the sonnet on the sonnet' (191). Autoeroticism on this scale, decently tempered with self-parody, shows just how confident the sonnet has become.

English Sonnets

1 Some fowls there be that have so perfect sight

Some fowls there be that have so perfect sight
Again the sun their eyes for to defend;
And some because the light doth them offend
Do never 'pear but in the dark or night.
Others rejoice that see the fire bright
And ween to play in it, as they do pretend,
And find the contrary of it that they intend.
Alas, of that sort I may be by right,
For to withstand her look I am not able
And yet can I not hide me in no dark place,
Remembrance so followeth me of that face.
So that with teary eyen, swollen and unstable,
My destiny to behold her doth me lead,
Yet do I know I run into the gleed.

THOMAS WYATT

2 My galley, chargèd with forgetfulness

My galley, chargèd with forgetfulness,
Thorough sharpe seas in winter nights doth pass
'Tween rock and rock; and eke my foe, alas,
That is my lord, steereth with cruelness;
And every hour, a thought in readiness,
As though that death were light in such a case;
An endless wind doth tear the sail apace
Of forcèd sighs, and trusty fearfulness;
A rain of tears, a cloud of dark disdain,
Hath done the wearied cords great hinderance;
Wreathèd with error and eke with ignorance,
The stars be hid that led me to this pain.
Drowned is reason that should me comfort,
And I remain, despairing of the port.

THOMAS WYATT

3   A Vow to Love Faithfully, Howsoever he be Rewarded

Set me whereas the sun doth parch the green
   Or where his beams do not dissolve the ice;
In temperate heat, where he is felt and seen;
   In presence prest of people, mad or wise;
Set me in high, or yet in low degree;
   In longest night, or in the shortest day;
In clearest sky, or where clouds thickest be;
   In lusty youth, or when my hairs are grey;
Set me in heaven, in earth, or else in hell,
   In hill, or dale, or in the foaming flood;
Thrall, or at large, alive whereso I dwell,
   Sick, or in health, in evil fame or good,
Hers will I be; and only with this thought
Content myself, although my chance be nought

HENRY HOWARD, EARL OF SURREY

4   Coming to kiss her lips

Coming to kiss her lips, (such grace I found)
   Me seemed I smelt a garden of sweet flowers:
That dainty odours from them threw around
   For damsels fit to deck their lovers' bowers.
   Her lips did smell like unto gillyflowers,
Her ruddy cheeks like unto roses red:
   Her snowy brows like budded bellamoures,
Her lovely eyes like pinks but newly spread.
Her goodly bosom like a strawberry bed,
   Her neck like to a bunch of colombines:
Her breast like lilies, ere their leaves be shed,
   Her nipples like young blossomed jessamines.
Such fragrant flowers do give most odorous smell,
But her sweet odour did them all excell.

EDMUND SPENSER

5   Was it a dream, or did I see it plain?

Was it a dream, or did I see it plain?
   A goodly table of pure ivory,
All spread with junkets, fit to entertain
   The greatest Prince with pompous royalty:
'Mongst which, there in a silver dish did lie
   Two golden apples of unvalued price,
Far passing those which Hercules came by,
   Or those which Atalanta did entice;
Exceeding sweet, yet void of sinful vice;
   That many sought, yet none could ever taste;
Sweet fruit of pleasure, brought from Paradise
   By Love himself, – and in his garden placed.
Her breast that table was, so richly spread,
My thoughts the guests, which would thereon have fed.

EDMUND SPENSER

6   Like as a huntsman after weary chase

Like as a huntsman after weary chase,
   Seeing the game from him escaped away,
Sits down to rest him in some shady place,
   With panting hounds beguiled of their prey:
   So after long pursuit and vain assay,
When I all weary had the chase forsook,
   The gentle deer returned the self-same way,
Thinking to quench her thirst at the next brook.
There she beholding me with milder look,
   Sought not to fly, but fearless still did bide:
Till I in hand her yet half trembling took,
   And with her own goodwill her firmly tied.
Strange thing me seemed to see a beast so wild,
So goodly won with her own will beguiled.

EDMUND SPENSER

7   One day I wrote her name upon the strand

One day I wrote her name upon the strand,
    But came the waves and washed it away:
Again I wrote it with a second hand,
    But came the tide, and made my pains his prey.
    Vain man, said she, that dost in vain assay,
A mortal thing so to immortalise,
    But I myself shall like to this decay,
And eke my name be wiped out likewise.
Not so (quod I), let baser things devise
    To die in dust, but you shall live by fame:
My verse your virtues rare shall eternise,
    And in the heavens write your glorious name.
Where whenas death shall all the world subdue,
Our love shall live, and later life renew.

EDMUND SPENSER

8   The Bargain

My true love hath my heart, and I have his,
    By just exchange, one for the other given.
I hold his dear, and mine he cannot miss,
    There never was a better bargain driven.
His heart in me keeps me and him in one,
    My heart in him his thoughts and senses guides;
He loves my heart, for once it was his own,
    I cherish his, because in me it bides.
His heart his wound received from my sight,
    My heart was wounded with his wounded heart;
For as from me on him his hurt did light,
    So still methought in me his hurt did smart.
Both equal hurt, in this change sought our bliss:
My true love hath my heart and I have his.

PHILIP SIDNEY

9 With how sad steps, O Moon, thou climbst the skies

With how sad steps, O Moon, thou climbst the skies,
   How silently, and with how wan a face,
   What, may it be that even in heav'nly place
That busy archer his sharp arrows tries?
Sure, if that long-with-love-acquainted eyes
   Can judge of Love, thou feelst a Lover's case;
   I read it in thy looks, thy languisht grace,
To me that feel the like, thy state descries.
   Then even of fellowship, O Moon, tell me, –
Is constant love deem'd there but want of wit?
   Are Beauties there as proud as here they be?
Do they above love to be loved, and yet
   Those lovers scorn whom that Love doth possess?
   Do they call virtue there ungratefulness?

PHILIP SIDNEY

10 Beauty, sweet Love, is like the morning dew

Beauty, sweet Love, is like the morning dew
   Whose short refresh upon the tender green
Cheers for a time, but till the sun doth shew
   And straight 'tis gone as it had never been.
Soon doth it fade that makes the fairest flourish,
   Short is the glory of the blushing rose,
The hue which thou so carefully dost nourish,
   Yet which at length thou must be forced to lose.
When thou, surcharged with burthen of thy years,
   Shalt bend thy wrinkles homeward to the earth,
And that, in beauty's lease expired, appears
   The date of age, the Kalends of our death –
But ah, no more! this must not be foretold,
For women grieve to think they must be old.

SAMUEL DANIEL

11   When winter snows upon thy sable hairs

When winter snows upon thy sable hairs,
   And frost of age hath nipped thy beauties near,
When dark shall seem thy day that never clears,
   And all lies withered that was held so dear,
Then take this picture which I here present thee,
   Limned with a pencil not all unworthy;
Here see the gifts that God and nature lent thee,
   Here read thyself and what I suffered for thee.
This may remain thy lasting monument,
   Which happily posterity may cherish;
These colours with thy fading are not spent,
   These may remain when thou and I shall perish.
If they remain, then thou shalt live thereby;
They will remain, and so thou canst not die.

SAMUEL DANIEL

12   Were I as base as is the lowly plain

Were I as base as is the lowly plain
   And you, my love, as high as heav'n above,
Yet should the thoughts of me your humble swain
   Ascend to heav'n in honour of my love.
Were I as high as heav'n above the plain,
   And you, my love, as humble and as low
As are the deepest bottoms of the main,
   Wheresoe'er you were, with you my love should go.
Were you the earth, dear love, and I the skies,
   My love should shine on you like to the sun,
And look upon you with ten thousand eyes,
   Till heav'n waxed blind and till the world were dun.
Wheresoe'er I am, below or else above you,
Wheresoe'er you are, my heart shall truly love you.

JOSHUA SYLVESTER

13 Of his Mistress upon Occasion of her Walking in a Garden

My Lady's presence makes the roses red
  Because to see her lips they blush for shame.
  The lilies' leaves for envy pale became
And her white hands in them this envy bred.
The marigold abroad the leaves did spread
  Because the sun's and her power is the same;
  The violet of purple colour came
Dyed with the blood she made my heart to shed.
  In brief, all flowers from her their virtue take;
From her sweet breath their sweet smells do proceed;
  The living heat which her eyebeams do make
Warmeth the ground and quickeneth the seed.
  The rain wherewith she watereth these flowers
  Falls from mine eyes which she dissolves in showers.

HENRY CONSTABLE

14 To God the Father

Great God, within whose simple essence we
  Nothing but that which is thyself can find:
  When on thyself thou did'st reflect thy mind
Thy thought was God, which took the form of thee:
And when this God thus born, thou lov'st, and he
  Loved thee again, with passion of like kind,
  (As lovers' sighs, which meet, become one wind)
Both breathed one spright of equal deity.
  Eternal father, whence these two do come
And wil'st the title of my father have,
As heavenly knowledge in my mind engrave,
  That it thy son's true image may become:
And cense my heart with sighs of holy Love,
That it the temple of the spright may prove.

HENRY CONSTABLE

15   Since there's no help, come let us kiss and part

Since there's no help, come let us kiss and part:
   Nay, I have done; you get no more of me;
And I am glad, yea, glad with all my heart
   That thus so cleanly I myself can free.
Shake hands forever; cancel all our vows;
   And when we meet at any time again,
Be it not seen in either of our brows
   That we one jot of former love retain.
Now at the last gasp of love's latest breath
   When, his pulse failing, passion speechless lies,
When faith is kneeling by his bed of death
   And innocence is closing up his eyes;
Now, if thou would'st, when all have given him over,
From Death to Life thou might'st him yet recover.

MICHAEL DRAYTON

16   Shall I compare thee to a summer's day?

Shall I compare thee to a summer's day?
   Thou art more lovely and more temperate:
Rough winds do shake the darling buds of May,
   And summer's lease hath all too short a date:
Sometime too hot the eye of heaven shines,
   And often is his gold complexion dimm'd;
And every fair from fair sometime declines,
   By chance or nature's changing course untrimm'd;
But thy eternal summer shall not fade,
   Nor lose possession of that fair thou owest;
Nor shall Death brag thou wanderest in his shade,
   When in eternal lines to time thou growest:
So long as men can breathe, or eyes can see,
So long lives this, and this gives life to thee.

WILLIAM SHAKESPEARE

17   When, in disgrace with fortune and men's eyes

When, in disgrace with fortune and men's eyes,
   I all alone beweep my outcast state,
And trouble deaf heaven with my bootless cries,
   And look upon myself, and curse my fate,
Wishing me like to one more rich in hope,
   Featured like him, like him with friends possessed,
Desiring this man's art and that man's scope,
   With what I most enjoy contented least;
Yet in these thoughts myself almost despising,
   Haply I think on thee, and then my state,
Like to the lark at break of day arising
   From sullen earth, sings hymns at heaven's gate;
For thy sweet love remembered such wealth brings
That then I scorn to change my state with kings.

                                  WILLIAM SHAKESPEARE

18   When to the sessions of sweet silent thought

When to the sessions of sweet silent thought
   I summon up remembrance of things past,
I sigh the lack of many a thing I sought,
   And with old woes new wail my dear time's waste:
Then can I drown an eye, unused to flow,
   For precious friends hid in death's dateless night,
And weep afresh love's long since cancelled woe,
   And moan the expense of many a vanished sight:
Then can I grieve at grievances foregone,
   And heavily from woe to woe tell o'er
The sad account of fore-bemoanèd moan,
   Which I new pay as if not paid before.
But if the while I think on thee, dear friend,
All losses are restored and sorrows end.

                                  WILLIAM SHAKESPEARE

19   Tired with all these, for restful death I cry

Tired with all these, for restful death I cry,
   As, to behold desert a beggar born,
And needy nothing trimmed in jollity,
   And purest faith unhappily forsworn,
And gilded honour shamefully misplaced,
   And maiden virtue rudely strumpeted,
And right perfection wrongfully disgraced,
   And strength by limping sway disabled,
And art made tongue-tied by authority,
   And folly, doctor-like, controlling skill,
And simple truth miscalled simplicity,
   And captive good attending captain ill:
Tired with all these, from these would I be gone,
Save that to die, I leave my love alone.

WILLIAM SHAKESPEARE

20   To me, fair friend, you never can be old

To me, fair friend, you never can be old,
   For as you were when first your eye I eyed,
Such seems your beauty still. Three winters cold
   Have from the forests shook three summers' pride,
Three beauteous springs to yellow autumn turned
   In process of the seasons have I seen,
Three April perfumes in three hot Junes burned,
   Since first I saw you fresh, which yet are green.
Ah, yet doth beauty, like a dial-hand,
   Steal from his figure, and no pace perceived;
So your sweet hue, which methinks still doth stand,
   Hath motion, and mine eye may be deceived:
For fear of which, hear this, thou age unbred;
Ere you were born was beauty's summer dead.

WILLIAM SHAKESPEARE

21   Let me not to the marriage of true minds

Let me not to the marriage of true minds
    Admit impediments. Love is not love
Which alters when it alteration finds,
    Or bends with the remover to remove:
O, no! it is an ever-fixèd mark,
    That looks on tempests and is never shaken;
It is the star to every wandering bark,
    Whose worth's unknown, although his height be taken.
Love's not Time's fool, though rosy lips and cheeks
    Within his bending sickle's compass come;
Love alters not with his brief hours and weeks,
    But bears it out even to the edge of doom.
If this be error and upon me proved,
I never writ, nor no man ever loved.

WILLIAM SHAKESPEARE

22   O thou, my lovely boy, who in thy power

O thou, my lovely boy, who in thy power
Dost hold Time's fickle glass, his sickle – hour;
    Who hast by waning grown, and therein showest
    Thy lovers withering as thy sweet self growest;
If Nature, sovereign mistress over wrack,
As thou goest onwards, still will pluck thee back,
    She keeps thee to this purpose, that her skill
    May time disgrace and wretched minutes kill.
Yet fear her, O thou minion of her pleasure!
She may detain, but not still keep, her treasure:
    Her audit, though delayed, answered must be,
    And her quietus is to render thee.

WILLIAM SHAKESPEARE

23   My mistress' eyes are nothing like the sun

My mistress' eyes are nothing like the sun;
   Coral is far more red than her lips' red:
If snow be white, why then her breasts are dun;
   If hairs be wires, black wires grow on her head.
I have seen roses damasked, red and white,
   But no such roses see I in her cheeks;
And in some perfumes is there more delight
   Than in the breath that from my mistress reeks.
I love to hear her speak, yet well I know
   That music hath a far more pleasing sound;
I grant I never saw a goddess go,
   My mistress, when she walks, treads on the ground:
And yet, by heaven, I think my love as rare
As any she belied with false compare.

WILLIAM SHAKESPEARE

24   Those lips that Love's own hand did make

Those lips that Love's own hand did make
   Breathed forth the sound that said 'I hate,'
To me that languished for her sake:
   But when she saw my woeful state,
Straight in her heart did mercy come,
   Chiding that tongue that ever sweet
Was used in giving gentle doom;
   And taught it thus anew to greet;
'I hate' she altered with an end,
   That followed it as gentle day
Doth follow night, who, like a fiend,
   From heaven to hell is flown away;
'I hate' from hate away she threw,
And saved my life, saying 'Not you.'

WILLIAM SHAKESPEARE

25   **From *Romeo and Juliet* (Act I, scene v)**

ROMEO [TO JULIET]
If I profane with my unworthiest hand
   This holy shrine, the gentle sin is this, –
My lips, two blushing pilgrims, ready stand,
   To smooth that rough touch with a tender kiss.

JULIET
Good pilgrim, you do wrong your hand too much
   Which mannerly devotion shows in this;
For saints have hands, that pilgrims' hands do touch,
   And palm to palm is holy palmer's kiss.

ROMEO
Have not saints lips, and holy palmers too?
JULIET
   Nay, pilgrim, lips that they must use in prayer.
ROMEO
O then, dear saint, let lips do what hands do;
   They pray, grant thou, lest faith turn to despair.

JULIET
Saints do not move, though grant for prayers' sake.
ROMEO [*kissing her*]
Then move not while my prayer's effect I take.

WILLIAM SHAKESPEARE

26 Thrice toss these oaken ashes in the air

Thrice toss these oaken ashes in the air,
    And thrice three times tie up this true-love's knot;
Thrice sit you down in this enchanted chair,
    And murmur soft, 'She will, or she will not.'
Go, burn those poisoned weeds in that blue fire,
    This cypress gathered out a dead man's grave,
These screech-owls' feathers and this prickling briar,
    That all thy thorny cares an end may have.
Then come, you fairies, dance with me a round:
    Dance in a circle, let my Love be centre!
Melodiously breathe an enchanted sound:
    Melt her hard heart, that some remorse may enter!
In vain are all the charms I can devise:
She hath an art to break them with her eyes.

THOMAS CAMPION

27 Death, be not proud

Death, be not proud, though some have called thee
    Mighty and dreadful, for, thou art not so,
    For, those, whom thou think'st thou dost overthrow,
Die not, poor death, nor yet canst thou kill me.
From rest and sleep, which but thy pictures be,
    Much pleasure, then from thee, much more must flow,
    And soonest our best men with thee doe go,
Best of their bones, and souls' delivery.
    Thou art slave to Fate, Chance, kings, and desperate men,
And dost with poison, war, and sickness dwell,
And poppy, or charms can make us sleep as well,
    And better than thy stroke. Why swell'st thou then?
One short sleep past, we wake eternally,
And death shall be no more; death, thou shalt die.

JOHN DONNE

28 At the round earth's imagined corners, blow

At the round earth's imagined corners, blow
   Your trumpets, Angels; and arise, arise
   From death, you numberless infinities
Of souls, and to your scattered bodies go,
All whom the flood did, and fire shall o'erthrow,
   All whom war, dearth, age, agues, tyrannies,
   Despair, law, chance, hath slain, and you whose eyes
Shall behold God, and never taste death's woe.
   But let them sleep, Lord, and me mourn a space.
For, if above all these my sins abound,
   'Tis late to ask abundance of thy grace,
When we are there; here on this lowly ground,
   Teach me how to repent; for that's as good
   As if thou hadst sealed my pardon with thy blood.

JOHN DONNE

29 Batter my heart, three-personed God

Batter my heart, three-personed God; for you
   As yet but knock, breathe, shine, and seek to mend.
   That I may rise and stand, o'erthrow me, and bend
Your force to break, blow, burn, and make me new.
I, like an usurped town to another due,
   Labour to admit you, but Oh, to no end.
   Reason, your viceroy in me, me should defend,
But is captived, and proves weak or untrue.
   Yet dearly I love you and would be lovèd fain,
But am betrothed unto your enemy.
   Divorce me, untie, or break that knot again,
Take me to you, imprison me, for I,
   Except you enthrall me, never shall be free,
   Nor ever chaste, except you ravish me.

JOHN DONNE

30　To my Book

It will be looked for, book, when some but see
Thy title, *Epigrams*, and named of me,
　　Thou should'st be bold, licentious, full of gall,
　　Wormwood, and sulphur, sharp, and toothed withal;
Become a petulant thing, hurl ink, and wit,
As madmen stones: not caring whom they hit.
　　Deceive their malice, who could wish it so.
　　And by thy wiser temper, let men know
Thou art not covetous of least self-fame,
Made from the hazard of another's shame:
　　Much less with lewd, profane, and beastly phrase,
　　To catch the world's loose laughter, or vain gaze.
He that departs with his own honesty
For vulgar praise, doth it too dearly buy.

BEN JONSON

31　To Anthea

Ah my Anthea! Must my heart still break?
(Love makes me write, what shame forbids to speak.)
　　Give me a kiss, and to that kiss a score;
　　Then to that twenty, add an hundred more:
A thousand to that hundred: so kiss on,
To make that thousand up a million.
　　Treble that million, and when that is done,
　　Let's kiss afresh, as when we first begun.
But yet, though love likes well such scenes as these,
There is an act that will more fully please:
　　Kissing and glancing, soothing, all make way
　　But to the acting of this private play:
Name it I would; but being blushing red,
The rest I'll speak when we both meet in bed.

ROBERT HERRICK

32   Dean Bourn, a Rude River in Devon, by which Sometimes he Lived

Dean Bourn, farewell; I never look to see
Dean, or thy warty incivility.
   Thy rocky bottom, that doth tear thy streams
   And makes them frantic, ev'n to all extremes;
To my content, I never should behold,
Were thy streams silver, or thy rocks all gold.
   Rocky thou art; and rocky we discover
   Thy men; and rocky are thy ways all over.
O men, O manners; now, and ever known
To be a rocky generation!
   A people currish; churlish as the seas;
   And rude (almost) as rudest savages.
With whom I did, and may re-sojourn when
Rocks turn to rivers, rivers turn to men.

ROBERT HERRICK

33   Sin

Lord, with what care hast thou begirt us round!
   Parents first season us: then schoolmasters
Deliver us to laws; they send us bound
   To rules of reason, holy messengers,
Pulpits and Sundays, sorrow dogging sin,
   Afflictions sorted, anguish of all sizes,
Fine nets and stratagems to catch us in,
   Bibles laid open, millions of surprises,
Blessings beforehand, ties of gratefulness,
   The sound of glory ringing in our ears;
Without, our shame; within, our consciences;
   Angels and grace, eternal hopes and fears.
Yet all these fences and their whole array
One cunning bosom-sin blows quite away.

GEORGE HERBERT

34   On his Blindness

When I consider how my light is spent
   Ere half my days, in this dark world and wide,
   And that one talent which is death to hide
Lodged with me useless, though my soul more bent
To serve therewith my Maker, and present
   My true account, lest He returning chide, –
   Doth God exact day-labour, light denied?
I fondly ask: – But Patience, to prevent
   That murmur, soon replies; God doth not need
Either man's work, or His own gifts: who best
   Bear His mild yoke, they serve Him best: His state
Is kingly; thousands at His bidding speed
   And post o'er land and ocean without rest:
They also serve who only stand and wait.

JOHN MILTON

35   On the Late Massacre in Piedmont

Avenge, O Lord, thy slaughtered saints, whose bones
   Lie scattered on the Alpine mountains cold,
   Even them who kept thy truth so pure of old
When all our fathers worshipped stocks and stones,
Forget not; in thy book record their groans
   Who were thy sheep, and in their ancient fold
   Slain by the bloody Piedmontese that rolled
Mother with infant down the rocks. Their moans
   The vales redoubled to the hills, and they
To heaven. Their martyred blood and ashes sow
   O'er all the Italian fields, where still doth sway
The triple tyrant, that from these may grow
   A hundredfold, who, having learnt thy way,
Early may fly the Babylonian woe.

JOHN MILTON

36   On his Having Arrived at the Age of Twenty-three

How soon hath Time, the subtle thief of youth,
   Stolen on his wing my three-and-twentieth year!
   My hasting days fly on with full career,
But my late spring no bud or blossom shew'th.
Perhaps my semblance might deceive the truth
   That I to manhood am arrived so near;
   And inward ripeness doth much less appear,
That some more timely-happy spirits endu'th.
   Yet, be it less or more, or soon or slow,
It shall be still in strictest measure even
   To that same lot, however mean or high,
Toward which Time leads me, and the will of Heaven;
   All is, if I have grace to use it so,
As ever in my great Task-Master's eye.

JOHN MILTON

37   On a Fair Beggar

Barefoot and ragged, with neglected hair,
She whom the Heavens at once made poor and fair,
   With humble voice and moving words did stay,
   To beg an alms of all who passed that way.
But thousands viewing her became her prize,
Willingly yielding to her conquering eyes,
   And caught by her bright hairs, whilst careless she
   Makes them pay homage to her poverty.
So mean a boon, said I, what can extort
From that fair mouth, where wanton Love to sport
   Amidst the pearls and rubies we behold?
Nature on thee has all her treasures spread,
Do but incline thy rich and precious head,
   And those fair locks shall pour down showers of gold.

PHILIP AYRES

38   Cynthia Sleeping in a Garden

Near a cool fountain, on a rose-bed lay
  My Cynthia, sleeping in the open air;
  Whom Sol espied, and seeing her so fair,
Gaz'd, till his wanton coursers lost their way.
  The proudest flowers were not asham'd to find
Their scent and colour rivall'd in her face;
Her bright curl'd hairs were toss'd from place to place,
  On neck and bosom by the amorous wind.
Her smiles were animated by her breath,
Which still as soon as born receiv'd their death,
  Being mortal made in pity to men's hearts:
Poor Lovers then did lie and take their rest,
For the Blind Boy who does our peace molest,
  Had in her sleeping eyes hid all his darts.

PHILIP AYRES

39   An Ode of Anacreon

My hairs are hoary, wrinkled is my Face,
I lose my strength, and all my manly grace;
  My eyes grow dim, my teeth are broke or gone,
  And the best part of all my life is done;
I'm drown'd in cares, and often sigh and weep;
My spirits fail me, broken is my sleep,
  Thoughts of the gaping grave distract my head;
  For in its paths, 'wake or asleep, we tread;
None can from it by art their feet restrain
Nor back, tho' wide its gates, can come again.
  Then since these ills attend the life of man,
  Let's make their burden easy as we can.
Cares are no cares, but whilst on them we think,
To clear our minds of such dull thoughts, let's drink.

PHILIP AYRES

40 Against Marriage

Out of mere love and arrant devotion,
Of marriage I'll give you this galloping notion:
   It's the bane of all business, the end of all pleasure,
   The consumption of youth, wit, courage, and treasure.
It's the rack of our thoughts, and the nightmare of sleep,
That sets us to work before the day peep.
   It makes us make brick without stubble or straw,
   And a cunt has no sense of conscience or law.
If you'd use flesh in the way that is noble,
In a generous wench there is nothing of trouble.
   You go on, you come off, say, do what you please –
   The worst you can fear is but a disease;
And diseases, you know, do admit of a cure,
But the hell-fire of marriage, none can endure.

JOHN WILMOT, EARL OF ROCHESTER

41 On the Death of Mr Richard West

In vain to me the smiling mornings shine
   And reddening Phoebus lifts his golden fire:
The birds in vain their amorous descant join;
   Or cheerful fields resume their green attire,
These ears, alas! for other notes repine,
   A different object do these eyes require:
My lonely anguish melts no heart but mine;
   And in my breast the imperfect joys expire.
Yet morning smiles the busy race to cheer,
   And new-born pleasure brings to happier men:
The fields to all their wonted tribute bear:
   To warm their little loves the birds complain:
I fruitless mourn to him that cannot hear,
   And weep the more, because I weep in vain.

THOMAS GRAY

42   To Mary Unwin

Mary! I want a lyre with other strings,
   Such aid from heaven as some have feigned they drew,
   An eloquence scarce given to mortals, new
And undebased by praise of meaner things,
That ere through age or woe I shed my wings
   I may record thy worth with honour due,
   In verse as musical as thou art true,
Verse that immortalises whom it sings: –
   But thou hast little need. There is a Book
By seraphs writ with beams of heavenly light,
   On which the eyes of God not rarely look,
A chronicle of actions just and bright –
   There all thy deeds, my faithful Mary, shine;
   And since thou own'st that praise, I spare thee mine.

WILLIAM COWPER

43   A Sonnet upon Sonnets

Fourteen, a sonneteer thy praises sings,
   What magic mysteries in that number lie!
Your hen hath fourteen eggs beneath her wings
   That fourteen chickens to the roost may fly.
Fourteen full pounds the jockey's stone must be;
   His age fourteen – a horse's prime is past.
   Fourteen long hours too oft the Bard must fast;
Fourteen bright bumpers – bliss he ne'er must see!
   Before fourteen, a dozen yields the strife;
Before fourteen – e'en thirteen's strength is vain.
   Fourteen good years – a woman gives us life;
Fourteen good men – we lose that life again.
   What lucubrations can be more upon it?
   Fourteen good measur'd verses make a sonnet.

ROBERT BURNS

44   Composed upon Westminster Bridge

Earth has not anything to show more fair:
   Dull would he be of soul who could pass by
   A sight so touching in its majesty:
This City now doth, like a garment, wear
The beauty of the morning; silent, bare,
   Ships, towers, domes, theatres, and temples lie
   Open unto the fields, and to the sky;
All bright and glittering in the smokeless air.
   Never did sun more beautifully steep
In his first splendour, valley, rock, or hill;
   Ne'er saw I, never felt, a calm so deep!
The river glideth at his own sweet will:
   Dear God! the very houses seem asleep;
And all that mighty heart is lying still!

WILLIAM WORDSWORTH

45   The world is too much with us

The world is too much with us; late and soon,
   Getting and spending, we lay waste our powers:
   Little we see in Nature that is ours;
We have given our hearts away, a sordid boon!
This Sea that bares her bosom to the moon;
   The winds that will be howling at all hours,
   And are up-gathered now like sleeping flowers;
For this, for everything, we are out of tune;
   It moves us not. – Great God! I'd rather be
A Pagan suckled in a creed outworn;
   So might I, standing on this pleasant lea,
Have glimpses that would make me less forlorn;
   Have sight of Proteus rising from the sea;
Or hear old Triton blow his wreathed horn.

WILLIAM WORDSWORTH

46   Nuns fret not at their convent's narrow room

Nuns fret not at their convent's narrow room;
   And hermits are contented with their cells;
   And students with their pensive citadels;
Maids at the wheel, the weaver at his loom,
Sit blithe and happy; bees that soar for bloom,
   High as the highest Peak of Furness-fells,
   Will murmur by the hour in foxglove bells;
In truth the prison, unto which we doom
   Ourselves, no prison is: and hence for me,
In sundry moods, 'twas pastime to be bound
Within the Sonnet's scanty plot of ground;
   Pleased if some Souls (for such there needs must be)
   Who have felt the weight of too much liberty,
Should find brief solace there, as I have found.

WILLIAM WORDSWORTH

47   With ships the sea was sprinkled far and nigh

With ships the sea was sprinkled far and nigh,
   Like stars in heaven, and joyously it showed;
   Some lying fast at anchor in the road,
Some veering up and down, one knew not why.
A goodly vessel did I then espy
   Come like a giant from a haven broad;
   And lustily along the bay she strode.
'Her tackling rich, and of apparel high',
   This ship was nought to me, nor I to her,
Yet I pursued her with a lover's look;
   This ship to all the rest did I prefer:
When will she turn, and whither? She will brook
   No tarrying; where she comes the winds must stir:
On went she, – and due north her journey took.

WILLIAM WORDSWORTH

48   Great men have been among us

Great men have been among us; hands that penned
   And tongues that uttered wisdom – better none:
   The later Sidney, Marvel, Harrington,
Young Vane, and others who called Milton friend.
These moralists could act and comprehend:
   They knew how genuine glory was put on;
   Taught us how rightfully a nation shone
In splendour: what strength was, that would not bend
   But in magnanimous meekness. France, 'tis strange,
Hath brought forth no such souls as we had then.
   Perpetual emptiness! unceasing change!
No single volume paramount, no code,
No master spirit, no determined road;
   But equally a want of books and men!

WILLIAM WORDSWORTH

49   Mutability

From low to high doth dissolution climb,
   And sinks from high to low, along a scale
   Of awful notes, whose concord shall not fail;
A musical but melancholy chime,
Which they can hear who meddle not with crime,
   Nor avarice, nor over-anxious care.
   Truths fails not; but her outward forms that bear
The longest date do melt like frosty rime,
   That in the morning whitened hill and plain
And is no more; drop like the tower sublime
   Of yesterday, which royally did wear
Its crown of weeds, but could not even sustain
   Some casual shout that broke the silent air,
Or the unimaginable touch of time.

WILLIAM WORDSWORTH

50   **To Toussaint L'Ouverture**

Toussaint, the most unhappy man of men!
   Whether the whistling rustic tend his plough
   Within thy hearing, or thy head be now
Pillowed in some deep dungeon's earless den;
O miserable chieftain! where and when
   Wilt thou find patience? Yet die not! do thou
   Wear rather in thy bonds a cheerful brow:
Though fallen thyself, never to rise again,
   Live, and take comfort. Thou hast left behind
Powers that will work for thee, air, earth, and skies:
   There's not a breathing of the common wind
That will forget thee; thou hast great allies;
Thy friends are exultations, agonies,
   And love, and man's unconquerable mind.

WILLIAM WORDSWORTH

51   **Milton**

Milton! Thou shouldst be living at this hour:
   England hath need of thee: she is a fen
   Of stagnant waters: altar, sword and pen,
Fireside, the heroic wealth of hall and bower,
Have forfeited their ancient English dower
   Of inward happiness. We are selfish men;
   O raise us up, return to us again,
And give us manners, virtue, freedom, power!
   Thy star was like a star, and dwelt apart;
Thou hadst a voice whose sound was like the sea;
Pure as the naked heavens, majestic, free,
   So didst thou travel on life's common way,
In cheerful godliness; and yet thy heart
   The lowliest duties on herself did lay.

WILLIAM WORDSWORTH

52 **Scorn not the sonnet**

Scorn not the Sonnet; Critic, you have frowned,
   Mindless of its just honours; with this key
   Shakespeare unlocked his heart; the melody
Of this small lute gave ease to Petrarch's wound;
A thousand times this pipe did Tasso sound;
   With it Camoëns soothed an exile's grief;
   The Sonnet glittered a gay myrtle leaf
Amid the cypress with which Dante crowned
   His visionary brow: a glow-worm lamp,
It cheered mild Spenser, called from Faery-land
   To struggle through dark ways; and, when a damp
Fell round the path of Milton, in his hand
   The Thing became a trumpet; whence he blew
   Soul-animating strains – alas, too few!

WILLIAM WORDSWORTH

53 **'With how sad steps,**
O Moon, thou climb'st the sky'

'With how sad steps, O Moon, thou climb'st the sky,
   How silently, and with how wan a face!'
Where art thou? Thou so often seen on high,
   Running among the clouds a Wood-nymph's race!
Unhappy Nuns, whose common breath's a sigh
   Which they would stifle, move at such a pace!
   The northern Wind, to call thee to the chase,
Must blow tonight his bugle-horn. Had I
   The power of Merlin, Goddess! this should be:
And all the stars, fast as the clouds were riven,
   Should sally forth, to keep thee company,
Hurrying and sparkling through the clear blue heaven;
But, Cynthia! should to thee the palm be given,
   Queen both for beauty and for majesty.

WILLIAM WORDSWORTH

54 Surprised by joy

Surprised by joy – impatient as the Wind
   I turned to share the transport – Oh! with whom
   But Thee, deep buried in the silent tomb,
That spot which no vicissitude can find?
Love, faithful love, recalled thee to my mind –
   But how could I forget thee? Through what power,
   Even for the least division of an hour,
Have I been so beguiled as to be blind
   To my most grievous loss! – That thought's return
Was the worst pang that sorrow ever bore,
   Save one, one only, when I stood forlorn,
Knowing my heart's best treasure was no more;
   That neither present time, nor years unborn
Could to my sight that heavenly face restore.

WILLIAM WORDSWORTH

55 Occasioned by the Battle of Waterloo.
February 1816

Intrepid sons of Albion! not by you
   Is life despised; ah, no, the spacious earth
   Ne'er saw a race who held, by right of birth,
So many objects to which love is due.
Ye slight not life – to God and nature true;
   But death, becoming death, is dearer far,
   When duty bids you bleed in open war:
Hence hath your prowess quelled that impious crew,
   Heroes! for instant sacrifice prepared,
Yet filled with ardour, and on triumph bent,
'Mid direst shocks of mortal accident,
   To You who fell, and you whom slaughter spared,
To guard the fallen, and consummate the event,
Your country rears this sacred monument!

WILLIAM WORDSWORTH

56   **To Mrs Siddons**

As when a child on some long winter's night,
    Affrighted clinging to its Grandam's knees,
With eager wondering and perturbed delight
    Listens strange tales of fearful dark decrees
Muttered to wretch by necromantic spell;
    Or of those hags, who at the witching time
    Of murky midnight ride the air sublime,
And mingle foul embrace with fiends of Hell.
    Cold Horror drinks its blood! Anon the tear
More gentle starts, to hear the Beldame tell
    Of pretty babes, that loved each other dear,
Murdered by cruel Uncle's mandate fell:
    Ev'n such the shivering joys thy tones impart,
    Ev'n so thou, Siddons! meltest my sad heart.

SAMUEL TAYLOR COLERIDGE

57   **Work Without Hope**

All nature seems at work. Stags leave their lair –
    The bees are stirring – birds are on the wing –
And winter slumbering in the open air,
    Wears on his smiling face a dream of spring!
And I, the while, the sole unbusy thing,
Nor honey make, nor pair, nor build, nor sing.
    Yet well I ken the banks where Amaranths blow,
    Have traced the fount whence streams of nectar flow.
Bloom, O ye Amaranths! bloom for whom ye may,
For me ye bloom not! Glide, rich streams, away!
    With lips unbrightened, wreathless brow, I stroll.
    And would you learn the spells that drowse my soul?
Work without hope draws nectar in a sieve,
And hope without an object cannot live.

SAMUEL TAYLOR COLERIDGE

58   To a Friend who Asked, How I Felt when the Nurse Presented my Infant to Me

Charles! My slow heart was only sad, when first
  I scanned that face of feeble infancy:
For dimly on my thoughtful spirit burst
  All I had been, and all my child might be!
But when I saw it on its mother's arm,
  And hanging at her bosom (she the while
  Bent o'er its features with a tearful smile)
Then I was thrilled and melted, and most warm
  Impressed a father's kiss: and all beguiled
Of dark remembrance and presageful fear,
I seemed to see an angel-form appear –
  'Twas even thine, beloved woman mild!
So for the mother's sake the child was dear,
  And dearer was the mother for the child.

SAMUEL TAYLOR COLERIDGE

59   High in the air exposed

High in the air exposed the slave is hung,
  To all the birds of heaven, their living food!
He groans not, though awaked by that fierce sun
  New torturers live to drink their parent blood;
He groans not, though the gorging vulture tear
  The quivering fibre. Hither look, O ye
  Who tore this man from peace and liberty!
Look hither, ye who weigh with politic care
  The gain against the guilt! Beyond the grave
There is another world: bear ye in mind,
Ere your decree proclaims to all mankind
  The gain is worth the guilt, that there the Slave,
Before the Eternal, thunder-tongued shall plead
Against the deep damnation of your deed.

ROBERT SOUTHEY

60   In these days, every mother's son or daughter

In these days, every mother's son or daughter
   Writes verse, which no one reads except the writer,
   Although, uninked, the paper would be whiter,
And worth, per ream, a hare, when you have caught her.
Hundreds of unstaunched Shelleys daily water
   Unanswering dust, a thousand Wordsworths scribble;
   And twice a thousand Corn Law Rhymers dribble
Rhymed prose, unread. Hymners of fraud and slaughter,
   By cant called other names, alone find buyers –
Who buy, but read not. 'What a loss in paper',
   Groans each immortal of the host of sighers!
'What profanation of the midnight taper
   In expirations vile! But I write well,
   And wisely print. Why don't my poems sell?'

EBENEZER ELLIOTT

61   John. In the sound of that rebellious word

John. In the sound of that rebellious word
   There is brave music. Jack, and Jacobin,
   Are vulgar terms; law-linked to shame and sin,
They have a twang of Jack the Hangman's cord:
Yet John hath merit which can well afford
   To be called Jack's. By life's strange offs and ons!
   Glory hath had great dealings with the Johns,
Since history first awaked where fable snored.
   John Cade, John Huss, John Hampden, and John Knox!
Ay, these were the names of fellows who had will.
John Wilson's name, far sounded, sounds not ill;
   But how unlike John Milton's or John Locke's!
John Bright, like Locke and Milton, scorns paid sloth;
And Johnson might have liked to gibbet both.

EBENEZER ELLIOTT

62   Toy of the Titans!

Toy of the Titans! Tiny Harp! again
  I quarrel with the order of thy strings,
  Established by the law of sonnet-kings,
And used by giants who do nought in vain.
Was Petrarch, then, mistaken in the strain
    That charms Italia? Were they tasteless things
    That Milton wrought? And are they mutterings
Untuneful, that pay Wordsworth with pleased pain?
  No. But I see that tyrants come of slaves;
That states are won by rush of robbers' steel;
    And millions starved and tortured to their graves,
Because as they are taught men think and feel;
    Therefore, I change the sonnet's slavish notes
    For cheaper music, suited to my thoughts.

EBENEZER ELLIOTT

63   Poet vs Parson

A hireling's wages to the priest are paid;
  While lives and dies, in want and rags, the bard!
  But preaching ought to be its own reward,
And not a sordid, if an honest trade.
Paul, labouring proudly with his hands, arrayed
  Regenerated hearts in peace and love;
  And when, with power, they preached the mystic dove,
Penn, Barclay, Clarkson, asked not Mammon's aid.
  As, for its own sake, poetry is sweet
To poets – so, on tasks of mercy bound,
  Religion travels with unsandalled feet,
Making the flinty desert holy ground;
  And never will her triumph be complete
While one paid pilgrim upon earth is found.

EBENEZER ELLIOTT

64 To the Nile

It flows through old hushed Egypt and its sands,
   Like some grave mighty thought threading a dream;
   And times and things, as in that vision, seem
Keeping along it their eternal stands, –
Caves, pillars, pyramids, the shepherd bands
   That roamed through the young world, the glory extreme
   Of high Sesostris, and that southern beam,
The laughing queen that caught the world's great hands.
   Then comes a mightier silence, stern and strong,
   As of a world left empty of its throng,
And the void weighs on us; and then we wake,
   And hear the fruitful stream lapsing along,
'Twixt villages, and think how we shall take
Our own calm journey on for human sake.

                                        JAMES LEIGH HUNT

65 To a Fish

You strange, astonished-looking, angle-faced,
   Dreary-mouthed, gaping wretches of the sea,
   Gulping salt-water everlastingly,
Cold-blooded, though with red your blood be graced,
And mute, though dwellers in the roaring waste;
   And you, all shapes beside, that fishy be, –
   Some round, some flat, some long, all devilry,
Legless, unloving, infamously chaste; –
   O scaly, slippery, wet, swift, staring wights,
What is't ye do? What life lead? Eh, dull goggles?
   How do ye vary your vile days and nights?
How pass your Sundays? Are ye still but joggles
   In ceaseless wash? Still nought but gapes, and bites,
And drinks, and stares, diversified with boggles?

                                        JAMES LEIGH HUNT

66 A Fish Answers

Amazing monster! that, for aught I know,
  With the first sight of thee didst make our race
  For ever stare! O flat and shocking face,
Grimly divided from the breast below!
Thou that on dry land horribly dost go
  With a split body and most ridiculous pace,
  Prong after prong, disgracer of all grace,
Long-useless-finned, haired, upright, unwet, slow!
  O breather of unbreathable, sword-sharp air,
How canst exist? How bear thyself, thou dry
  And dreary sloth? What particle canst share
Of the only blessed life, the watery?
  I sometimes see of ye an actual *pair*
Go by! linked fin by fin! most odiously.

JAMES LEIGH HUNT

67 The Grasshopper and the Cricket

Green little vaulter in the sunny grass,
  Catching your heart up at the feel of June,
  Sole voice that's heard amidst the lazy noon,
When even the bees lag at the summoning brass;
And you, warm little housekeeper, who class
  With those who think the candles come too soon,
  Loving the fire, and with your tricksome tune
Nick the glad silent moments as they pass;
  Oh sweet and tiny cousins, that belong
One to the fields, the other to the hearth,
  Both have your sunshine; both, though small, are strong
At your clear hearts; and both were sent on earth
  To sing in thoughtful ears this natural song:
Indoors and out, summer and winter, Mirth.

JAMES LEIGH HUNT

68 To Lake Leman

Rousseau – Voltaire – our Gibbon – and De Staël –
   Leman! these names are worthy of thy shore,
   Thy shore of names like these! wert thou no more
Their memory thy remembrance would recall:
To them thy banks were lovely as to all,
   But they have made them lovelier, for the lore
   Of mighty minds doth hallow in the core
Of human hearts the ruin of a wall
   Where dwelt the wise and wondrous; but by *thee*
How much more, Lake of Beauty! do we feel
   In sweetly gliding o'er thy crystal sea,
The wide glow of that not ungentle zeal,
   Which of the heirs of immortality
Is proud, and makes the breath of glory real!

GEORGE GORDON, LORD BYRON

69 On the Castle of Chillon

Eternal Spirit of the chainless Mind!
   Brightest in dungeons, Liberty, thou art
   For there thy habitation is the heart –
The heart which love of Thee alone can bind;
And when thy sons to fetters are consigned,
   To fetters, and the damp vault's dayless gloom,
   Their country conquers with their martyrdom,
And Freedom's fame finds wings on every wind.
   Chillon! thy prison is a holy place
And thy sad floor an altar, for 'twas trod,
   Until his very steps have left a trace
Worn, as if thy cold pavement were a sod,
   By Bonnivard! May none those marks efface!
For they appeal from tyranny to God.

GEORGE GORDON, LORD BYRON

70 Ozymandias

I met a traveller from an antique land
　　Who said: Two vast and trunkless legs of stone
Stand in the desert . . . Near them, on the sand,
　　Half sunk, a shattered visage lies, whose frown,
And wrinkled lip, and sneer of cold command,
　　Tell that its sculptor well those passions read
Which yet survive, stamped on these lifeless things,
　　The hand that mocked them, and the heart that fed:
And on the pedestal these words appear:
　　'My name is Ozymandias, king of kings:
Look on my works, ye Mighty, and despair!'
　　Nothing beside remains. Round the decay
Of that colossal wreck, boundless and bare
　　The lone and level sands stretch far away.

PERCY BYSSHE SHELLEY

71 To the Nile

Month after month the gathered rains descend
　　Drenching yon secret Ethiopian dells,
　　And from the desert's ice-girt pinnacles
Where Frost and Heat in strange embraces blend
On Atlas, fields of moist snow half depend.
　　Girt there with blasts and meteors Tempest dwells
　　By Nile's aëreal urn, with rapid spells
Urging those waters to their mighty end.
　　O'er Egypt's land of Memory floods are level
And they are thine, O Nile – and well thou knowest
　　That soul-sustaining airs and blasts of evil
And fruits and Poisons spring where'er thou flowest.
　　Beware, O Man – for knowledge must to thee,
　　Like the great flood to Egypt, ever be.

PERCY BYSSHE SHELLEY

72 England in 1819

An old, mad, blind, despised, and dying king, –
    Princes, the dregs of their dull race, who flow
Through public scorn – mud from a muddy spring –
    Rulers who neither see, nor feel, nor know,
But leech-like to their fainting country cling,
    Till they drop, blind in blood, without a blow, –
A people starved and stabbed in the untilled field, –
    An army, which liberticide and prey
Makes as a two-edged sword to all who wield, –
    Golden and sanguine laws which tempt and slay;
Religion Christless, Godless – a book sealed;
A Senate, – Time's worst statute unrepealed, –
    Are graves, from which a glorious Phantom may
    Burst, to illumine our tempestuous day.

PERCY BYSSHE SHELLEY

73 To Wordsworth

Poet of Nature, thou hast wept to know
    That things depart which never may return:
Childhood and youth, friendship and love's first glow,
    Have fled like sweet dreams, leaving thee to mourn.
These common woes I feel. One loss is mine
    Which thou too feel'st, yet I alone deplore.
Thou wert as a lone star, whose light did shine
    On some frail bark – in winter's midnight roar:
Thou hast like to a rock-built refuge stood
Above the blind and battling multitude:
    In honoured poverty thy voice did weave
Songs consecrate to truth and liberty, –
    Deserting these, thou leavest me to grieve,
Thus having been, that thou shouldst cease to be.

PERCY BYSSHE SHELLEY

74   Ye hasten to the dead!

Ye hasten to the dead! What seek ye there,
  Ye restless thoughts and busy purposes
Of the idle brain, which the world's livery wear?
  O thou quick heart, which pantest to possess
All that pale Expectation feigneth fair!
  Thou vainly curious mind which wouldest guess
Whence thou didst come, and whither thou must go,
And ill that never yet was known would know –
  Oh, whither hasten ye, that thus ye press,
With such swift feet life's green and pleasant path,
  Seeking, alike from happiness and woe,
A refuge in the cavern of grey death?
  O heart, and mind, and thoughts! what thing do you
  Hope to inherit in the grave below?

PERCY BYSSHE SHELLEY

75   The barn door is open and ready to winnow

The barn door is open and ready to winnow,
The woodman is resting and getting his dinner
  And calls to the maiden with little to say
  Who takes the hot dinner and hurries away.
The hen's in the dust and the hog's in the dirt.
The mower is busy and stripped in his shirt,
  The waggon is empty and ready to start.
  The ploughman is merry and drinking his quart,
The men are at work and the schoolboy at play.
The maid's in the meadow a-making the hay;
  The ducks are a-feeding and running about,
  The hogs are a-noising and try to get out:
The dog's at his bone and the ass at his tether,
And cows in the pasture all feeding together.

JOHN CLARE

76   I dreaded walking where there was no path

I dreaded walking where there was no path
And pressed with cautious tread the meadow swath
   And always turned to look with wary eye
   And always feared the owner coming by;
Yet everything about where I had gone
Appeared so beautiful I ventured on
   And when I gained the road where all are free
   I fancied every stranger frowned at me
And every kinder look appeared to say
You've been on trespass in your walk today.
   I've often thought the day appeared so fine,
   How beautiful if such a place were mine;
But having nought I never feel alone
And cannot use another's as my own.

JOHN CLARE

77   The Gipsy Camp

The snow falls deep, the Forest lies alone:
The boy goes hasty for his load of brakes,
Then thinks upon the fire and hurries back;
The Gipsy knocks his hands and tucks them up,
And seeks his squalid camp, half hid in snow,
Beneath the oak, which breaks away the wind,
And bushes close, with snow like hovel warm:
There stinking mutton roasts upon the coals,
And the half-roasted dog squats close and rubs,
Then feels the heat too strong and goes aloof;
He watches well, but none a bit can spare,
And vainly waits the morsel thrown away:
   'Tis thus they live – a picture to the place;
   A quiet, pilfering, unprotected race.

JOHN CLARE

78   Memory

I would not that my being all should die
   And pass away with every common lot;
I would not that my humble dust should lie
    In quite a strange and unfrequented spot,
    By all unheeded and by all forgot,
With nothing save the heedless winds to sigh
   And nothing but the dewy morn to weep
About my grave, far hid from the world's eye.
I feign would have some friend to wander nigh
   And find a path to where my ashes sleep:
Not the cold heart that merely passes by
    To read who lieth there, but such that keep
Past memories warm with deeds of other years
And pay to friendship some few friendly tears.

JOHN CLARE

79   On First Looking into Chapman's Homer

Much have I travelled in the realms of gold,
   And many goodly states and kingdoms seen;
   Round many western islands have I been
Which bards in fealty to Apollo hold.
Oft of one wide expanse had I been told
   That deep-browed Homer ruled as his demesne;
   Yet did I never breathe its pure serene
Till I heard Chapman speak out loud and bold:
   Then felt I like some watcher of the skies
When a new planet swims into his ken;
   Or like stout Cortez, when with eagle eyes
He stared at the Pacific – and all his men
   Looked at each other with a wild surmise –
Silent, upon a peak in Darien.

JOHN KEATS

80   When I have fears that I may cease to be

When I have fears that I may cease to be
   Before my pen has gleaned my teeming brain,
Before high-pilèd books, in charact'ry,
   Hold like rich garners the full-ripen'd grain;
When I behold, upon the night's starred face,
   Huge cloudy symbols of a high romance,
And feel that I may never live to trace
   Their shadows, with the magic hand of chance;
And when I feel, fair creature of an hour!
   That I shall never look upon thee more,
Never have relish in the faery power
   Of unreflecting love! – then on the shore
Of the wide world I stand alone, and think,
Till Love and Fame to nothingness do sink.

JOHN KEATS

81   To Sleep

O soft embalmer of the still midnight!
   Shutting, with careful fingers and benign,
Our gloom-pleased eyes, embowered from the light,
   Enshaded in forgetfulness divine;
O soothest Sleep! if so it please thee, close,
   In midst of this thine hymn my willing eyes,
Or wait the amen, ere thy poppy throws
   Around my bed its lulling charities;
Then save me, or the passèd day will shine
   Upon my pillow, breeding many woes;
Save me from curious conscience, that still lords
   Its strength in darkness, burrowing like a mole;
Turn the key deftly in the oilèd wards,
   And seal the hushèd casket of my soul.

JOHN KEATS

82   Happy is England!

Happy is England! I could be content
   To see no other verdure than its own;
   To feel no other breezes than are blown
Through its tall woods with high romances blent:
Yet do I sometimes feel a languishment
   For skies Italian, and an inward groan
   To sit upon an Alp as on a throne,
And half forget what world or worldling meant.
   Happy is England, sweet her artless daughters;
Enough their simple loveliness for me,
   Enough their whitest arms in silence clinging:
Yet do I often warmly burn to see
   Beauties of deeper glance, and hear their singing,
And float with them about the summer waters.

JOHN KEATS

83   Sonnet Written on a Blank Page in Shakespeare's Poems

Bright star! would I were steadfast as thou art –
   Not in lone splendour hung aloft the night
And watching, with eternal lids apart,
   Like Nature's patient, sleepless Eremite,
The moving waters at their priest-like task
   Of pure ablution round earth's human shores,
Or gazing on the new soft fallen mask
   Of snow upon the mountains and the moors.
No – yet still steadfast, still unchangeable,
   Pillowed upon my fair love's ripening breast,
To feel for ever its soft fall and swell,
   Awake for ever in a sweet unrest,
Still, still to hear her tender-taken breath,
And so live ever – or else swoon to death.

JOHN KEATS

84 On the Sonnet

If by dull rhymes our English must be chained,
    And, like Andromeda, the Sonnet sweet
Fettered, in spite of pained loveliness;
    Let us find out, if we must be constrained,
Sandals more interwoven and complete
    To fit the naked foot of poesy;
Let us inspect the lyre, and weigh the stress
    Of every chord, and see what may be gained
By ear industrious, and attention meet;
    Misers of sound and syllable, no less
Than Midas of his coinage, let us be
    Jealous of dead leaves in the bay wreath crown;
So, if we may not let the Muse be free,
    She will be bound with garlands of her own.

JOHN KEATS

85 To a Friend

When we were idlers with the loitering rills,
    The need of human love we little noted:
    Our love was nature; and the peace that floated
On the white mist, and dwelt upon the hills,
To sweet accord subdued our wayward wills:
    One soul was ours, one mind, one heart devoted,
    That wisely doating asked not why it doated,
And ours the unknown joy which knowing kills.
    But now I find how dear thou wert to me;
That man is more than half of nature's treasure,
    Of that fair beauty which no eye can see,
Of that sweet music which no ear can measure;
And now the streams may sing for others' pleasure,
    The hills sleep on in their eternity.

HARTLEY COLERIDGE

86   Long time a child

Long time a child, and still a child, when years
   Had painted manhood on my cheek, was I;
   For yet I lived like one not born to die:
A thriftless prodigal of smiles and tears,
No hope I needed, and I knew no fears.
   But sleep, though sweet, is only sleep, and waking
   I waked to sleep no more, at once o'ertaking
The vanguard of my age, with all arrears
   Of duty on my back. Nor child, nor man,
Nor youth, nor sage, I find my head is grey;
   For I have lost the race I never ran:
A rathe December blights my lagging May,
   And still I am a child, though I be old:
   Time is my debtor for my years untold.

HARTLEY COLERIDGE

87   Think upon Death

Think upon Death, 'tis good to think of Death,
   But better far to think upon the Dead.
   Death is a spectre with a bony head,
Or the mere mortal body without breath,
The state foredoomed of every son of Seth,
   Decomposition – dust, or dreamless sleep.
   But the dear Dead are they for whom we weep,
For whom I credit all the Bible saith.
   Dead is my father, dead is my good mother,
And what on earth have I to do but die?
But if by grace I reach the blessed sky,
   I fain would see the same, and not another;
   The very father that I used to see,
   The mother that has nursed me on her knee.

HARTLEY COLERIDGE

88 Silence

There is a silence where hath been no sound,
   There is a silence where no sound may be,
   In the cold grave – under the deep deep sea,
Or in wide desert where no life is found,
Which hath been mute, and still must sleep profound;
   No voice is hushed – no life treads silently,
   But clouds and cloudy shadows wander free,
That never spoke, over the idle ground:
   But in green ruins, in the desolate walls
Of antique palaces, where Man hath been,
   Though the dun fox, or wild hyena, calls,
And owls, that flit continually between,
   Shriek to the echo, and the low winds moan,
   There the true Silence is, self-conscious and alone.

THOMAS HOOD

89 Death

It is not death, that sometime in a sigh
   This eloquent breath shall take its speechless flight;
That sometime these bright stars, that now reply
   In sunlight to the sun, shall set in night;
   That this warm conscious flesh shall perish quite,
And all life's ruddy springs forget to flow;
   That thoughts shall cease, and the immortal Sprite
Be lapped in alien clay and laid below;
It is not death to know this, – but to know
   That pious thoughts, which visit at new graves
In tender pilgrimage, will cease to go
   So duly and so oft, – and when grass waves
Over the past-away, there may be then
No resurrection in the minds of men.

THOMAS HOOD

90 **'Sweets to the sweet – Farewell'** (Hamlet)

Time was I liked a cheesecake well enough –
    All human children have a sweetish tooth;
I used to revel in a pie, or puff,
    Or tart – we all were Tartars in our youth;
To meet with jam or jelly was good luck,
    All candies most complacently I crumped,
A stick of liquorice was good to suck,
    And sugar was as often liked as lumped!
On treacle's 'linkèd sweetness long drawn out',
    Or honey I could feast like any fly;
I thrilled when lollipops were hawked about;
    How pleased to compass hard-bake or bull's-eye;
How charmed if Fortune in my power cast
Elecampane – but that campaign is past.

THOMAS HOOD

91 **A Crocodile**

Hard by the lilied Nile I saw
A duskish river dragon stretched along.
The brown habergeon of his limbs enamelled
With sanguine alamandines and rainy pearl:
And on his back there lay a young one sleeping,
No bigger than a mouse; with eyes like beads,
And a small fragment of its speckled egg
Remaining on its harmless, pulpy snout;
A thing to laugh at, as it gaped to catch
The baulking merry flies. In the iron jaws
Of the great devil-beast, like a pale soul
Fluttering in rocky hell, lightsomely flew
A snowy trochilus, with roseate beak
Tearing the hairy leeches from his throat.

THOMAS LOVELL BEDDOES

92   **To Tartar, a Terrier Beauty**

Snowdrop of dogs with ear of brownest dye
   Like the last orphan leaf of naked tree
   Which shudders in bleak autumn; though by thee,
Of hearing careless and untutored eye,
   Not understood articulate speech of men
Nor marked the artificial mind of books –
   The mortal's voice eternised by the pen –
Yet hast thou thought and language all unknown
   To Babel's scholars; oft intensest looks,
Long scrutiny over some dark-veined stone
   Dost thou bestow, learning dead mysteries
Of the world's birthday, oft in eager tone
   With quick-tailed fellows bandiest prompt replies,
   Solicitudes canine, four-footed amities.

THOMAS LOVELL BEDDOES

93   **To Night**

So thou art come again, old black-winged night,
   Like an huge bird, between us and the sun,
Hiding with outstretched form the genial light;
   And still beneath thine icy bosom's dun
And cloudy plumage hatching fog-breathed blight
   And embryo storms and crabbèd frosts, that shun
Day's warm caress. The owls from ivied loop
   Are shrieking homage, as thou towerest high;
Like sable crow pausing in eager stoop
   On the dim world thou gluttest thy clouded eye,
Silently waiting latest time's fell whoop,
   When thou shalt quit thine eyrie in the sky,
To pounce upon the world with eager claw,
And tomb time, death, and substance in thy maw.

THOMAS LOVELL BEDDOES

94 Go from me

Go from me. Yet I feel that I shall stand
    Henceforward in thy shadow. Nevermore
    Alone upon the threshold of my door
Of individual life, I shall command
The uses of my soul, nor lift my hand
    Serenely in the sunshine as before,
    Without the sense of that which I forbore . . .
Thy touch upon the palm. The widest land
    Doom takes to part us, leaves thy heart in mine
With pulses that beat double. What I do
    And what I dream includes thee, as the wine
Must taste of its own grape. And when I sue
    God for myself, He hears that name of thine,
And sees within my eyes, the tears of two.

ELIZABETH BARRETT BROWNING

95 When our two souls stand up erect and strong

When our two souls stand up erect and strong,
    Face to face, silent, drawing nigh and nigher,
    Until the lengthening wings break into fire
At either curved point, – what bitter wrong
Can the earth do to us that we should not long
    Be here contented? Think. In mounting higher,
    The angels would press on us and aspire
To drop some golden orb of perfect song
    Into our deep, dear silence. Let us stay
Rather on earth, Beloved, – where the unfit
    Contrarious moods of men recoil away
And isolate pure spirits, and permit
    A place to stand and love in for a day,
With darkness and the death-hour rounding it.

ELIZABETH BARRETT BROWNING

96   First time he kissed me

First time he kissed me, he but only kissed
   The fingers of this hand wherewith I write;
   And ever since, it grew more clean and white,
Slow to world-greetings, quick with its 'Oh, list',
When the angels speak. A ring of amethyst
   I could not wear here, plainer to my sight,
   Than that first kiss. The second passed in height
The first, and sought the forehead, and half missed,
   Half falling on the hair. O beyond meed!
That was the chrism of love, which love's own crown,
   With sanctifying sweetness, did precede.
The third upon my lips was folded down
   In perfect, purple state; since when, indeed,
I have been proud and said, 'My love, my own.'

ELIZABETH BARRETT BROWNING

97   How do I love thee?

How do I love thee? Let me count the ways,
   I love thee to the depth and breadth and height
   My soul can reach, when feeling out of sight
For the ends of Being and ideal Grace.
I love thee to the level of everyday's
   Most quiet need, by sun and candlelight.
   I love thee freely, as men strive for Right;
I love thee purely, as they turn from Praise.
   I love thee with the passion put to use
In my old griefs, and with my childhood's faith.
   I love thee with a love I seemed to lose
With my lost saints – I love thee with the breath,
   Smiles, tears, of all my life! – and, if God choose,
I shall but love thee better after death.

ELIZABETH BARRETT BROWNING

98   The Galaxy

Torrent of light and river of the air,
  Along whose bed the glimmering stars are seen
  Like gold and silver sands in some ravine
Where mountain streams have left their channels bare!
The Spaniard sees in thee the pathway, where
  His patron saint descended in the sheen
  Of his celestial armour, on serene
And quiet nights, when all the heavens were fair.
  Not this I see, nor yet the ancient fable
Of Phaeton's wild course, that scorched the skies
  Where'er the hoofs of his hot coursers trod;
But the white drift of worlds o'er chasms of sable,
  The stardust that is whirled aloft and flies
From the invisible chariot wheels of God.

HENRY WADSWORTH LONGFELLOW

99   Mezzo Cammin

Half of my life is gone, and I have let
  The years slip from me and have not fulfilled
  The aspiration of my youth, to build
Some tower of song with lofty parapet.
Not indolence, nor pleasure, nor the fret
  Of restless passions that would not be stilled,
  But sorrow, and a care that almost killed,
Kept me from what I may accomplish yet;
  Though, half-way up the hill I see the Past
Lying beneath me with its sounds and sights, –
  A city in the twilight dim and vast,
With smoking roofs, soft bells and gleaming lights, –
  And hear above me on the autumnal blast
The cataract of Death far thundering from the heights.

HENRY WADSWORTH LONGFELLOW

100   Shakespeare

A vision as of crowded city streets,
    With human life in endless overflow;
    Thunder of thoroughfares; trumpets that blow
To battle; clamour, in obscure retreats,
Of sailors landed from their anchored fleets;
    Tolling of bells in turrets, and below
    Voices of children and bright flowers that throw
O'er garden walls their intermingled sweets!
    This vision comes to me when I unfold
The volume of the poet paramount,
    Whom all the Muses loved, not one alone: –
Into his hands they put the lyre of gold,
    And, crowned with sacred laurel at their fount,
Placed him as Musagetes on their throne.

HENRY WADSWORTH LONGFELLOW

101   Chaucer

An old man in a lodge within a park;
    The chamber walls depicted all around
    With portraitures of huntsmen, hawk, and hound,
And the hurt deer. He listeneth to the lark,
Whose song comes with the sunshine through the dark
    Of painted glass in leaden lattice bound;
    He listeneth and he laugheth at the sound,
Then writeth in a book like any clerk.
    He is the poet of the dawn, who wrote
The Canterbury Tales, and his old age
    Made beautiful with song; and as I read
I hear the crowing cock, I hear the note
    Of lark and linnet, and from every page
Rise odours of ploughed field or flowery mead.

HENRY WADSWORTH LONGFELLOW

102   The Cross of Snow

In the long, sleepless watches of the night,
   A gentle face – the face of one long dead
   Looks at me from the wall, where round its head
The night-lamp casts a halo of pale light.
Here in this room she died; and soul more white
   Never through martyrdom of fire was led
   To its repose; nor can in books be read
The legend of a life more benedight.
   There is a mountain in the distant West
That, sun-defying, in its deep ravines
   Displays a cross of snow upon its side.
Such is the cross I wear upon my breast
   These eighteen years, through all the changing scenes
And seasons, changeless since the day she died.

HENRY WADSWORTH LONGFELLOW

103   The Kraken

Below the thunders of the upper deep;
   Far far beneath in the abysmal sea,
His ancient, dreamless, uninvaded sleep
   The Kraken sleepeth: faintest sunlights flee
About his shadowy sides: above him swell
   Huge sponges of millennial growth and height;
   And far away into the sickly light,
From many a wondrous grot and secret cell
   Unnumber'd and enormous polypi
Winnow with giant fins the slumbering green.
   There hath he lain for ages and will lie
Battening upon huge seaworms in his sleep,
Until the latter fire shall heat the deep;
   Then once by men and angels to be seen,
In roaring he shall rise and on the surface die.

ALFRED, LORD TENNYSON

104   Poets and their Bibliographies

Old poets foster'd under friendlier skies,
  Old Virgil who would write ten lines, they say,
  At dawn, and lavish all the golden day
To make them wealthier in the readers' eyes;
And you, old popular Horace, you the wise
  Adviser of the nine-years-ponder'd lay,
  And you, that wear a wreath of sweeter bay,
Catullus, whose dead songster never dies;
  If, glancing downward on the kindly sphere
That once had roll'd you round and round the sun,
  You see your Art still shrined in human shelves,
You should be jubilant that you flourish'd here
  Before the Love of Letters, overdone,
Had swamped the sacred poets with themselves.

ALFRED, LORD TENNYSON

105   Buonaparte

He thought to quell the stubborn hearts of oak,
  Madman! to chain with chains, and bind with bands
  That island queen who sways the floods and lands
From Ind to Ind, but in fair daylight woke,
  When from her wooden walls, – lit by sure hands, –
With thunders and with lightnings and with smoke, –
Peal after peal, the British battle broke,
  Lulling the brine against the Coptic sands.
We taught him lowlier moods, when Elsinore
  Heard the war moan along the distant sea,
Rocking with shattered spars, with sudden fires
  Flamed over: at Trafalgar yet once more
We taught him: late he learned humility
  Perforce, like those whom Gideon schooled with briars.

ALFRED, LORD TENNYSON

106   A Question by Shelley

'Then what is life?' I cried. From his rent deeps
   Of soul the poet cast that burning word;
   And it should seem as though his prayer was heard,
For he died soon; and now his rest he keeps
Somewhere with the great spirit who never sleeps!
   He had left us to murmur on awhile
   And question still most fruitlessly this pile
Of natural shows, What life is? Why man weeps?
   Why sins? – and whither when the awful veil
Floats on to him he sinks from earthly sight?
   Some are, who never grow a whit more pale
For thinking on the general mystery,
Ground of all being; yet may I rather be
   Of those who know and feel that it is night.

ALFRED, LORD TENNYSON

107   A Farewell to Poetry

Long hast thou wandered on the happy mountain
   Where the sweet Muses are for ever dwelling;
And by the waters of that hallowed fountain
   Which from earth's deep is musically welling;
Hast heard Apollo's ancient lips recounting
   Legends of gods too high for human telling,
Until thy heart its mortal bound surmounting
   Grew faint amid the pains of joy o'er-swelling.
Then wisely shalt thou leave the wizard places,
   That charming wisdom, and that voice melodious,
To seek a home not distant many paces,
   A peaceful home to weary souls commodious,
Where the meek son of our almighty lover
Stills every pang and bids all fear be over.

ALFRED, LORD TENNYSON

108   The Mute Lovers on the Railway Journey

They bade farewell; but neither spoke of love.
   The railway bore him off with rapid pace,
He gazed awhile on Edith's garden grove,
   Till alien woodlands overlapped the place –
Alas! he cried, how mutely did we part!
   I feared to test the truth I seemed to see.
Oh! that the love dream in her timid heart
   Had sighed itself awake, and called for me!
I could have answered with a ready mouth,
   And told a sweeter dream; but each forbore.
He saw the hedgerows fleeting to the north
On either side, whilst he look'd sadly forth:
   Then set himself to face the vacant south,
While fields and woods ran back to Edith More.

CHARLES TENNYSON-TURNER

109   Letty's Globe

When Letty had scarce passed her third glad year,
   And her young, artless words began to flow,
One day we gave the child a coloured sphere
   Of the wide earth, that she might mark and know,
By tint and outline, all its sea and land.
   She patted all the world; old empires peeped
Between her baby fingers; her soft hand
   Was welcome at all frontiers. How she leaped,
And laughed, and prattled in her world-wide bliss;
   But when we turned her sweet unlearned eye
   On our own isle, she raised a joyous cry,
'Oh! yes, I see it, Letty's home is there!'
   And, while she hid all England with a kiss,
Bright over Europe fell her golden hair.

CHARLES TENNYSON-TURNER

110   On Seeing a Little Child Spin a Coin
of Alexander the Great

This is the face of him, whose quick resource
    Of eye and hand subdued Bucephalus,
And made the shadow of a startled horse
    A foreground for his glory. It is thus
They hand him down; this coin of Philip's son
    Recalls his life, his glories, and misdeeds;
And that abortive court of Babylon,
    Where the world's throne was left among the reeds.
His dust is lost among the ancient dead,
    A coin his only presence: he is gone:
And all but this half mythic image fled –
    A simple child may do him shame and slight;
'Twixt thumb and finger take the golden head,
    And spin the horns of Ammon out of sight.

CHARLES TENNYSON-TURNER

111   The Quiet Tide Near Ardrossan

On to the beach the quiet waters crept:
    But, though I stood not far within the land,
    No tidal murmur reached me from the strand.
The mirrored clouds beneath old Arran slept.
    I looked again across the watery waste:
The shores were full, the tide was near its height,
    Though scarcely heard: the reefs were drowning fast,
And an imperial whisper told the might
    Of the outer floods, that pressed into the bay,
Though all besides was silent. I delight
In the rough billows, and the foam-ball's flight:
    I love the shore upon a stormy day;
But yet more stately were the power and ease
That with a whisper deepened all the seas.

CHARLES TENNYSON-TURNER

112 Silence

There are some qualities – some incorporate things,
  That have a double life, which thus is made
A type of that twin entity which springs
  From matter and light, evinced in solid and shade.
There is a two-fold Silence – sea and shore –
  Body and soul. One dwells in lonely places,
  Newly with grass o'ergrown; some solemn graces,
Some human memories and tearful lore,
Render him terrorless: his name's 'No More'.
  He is the corporate Silence: dread him not!
No power hath he of evil in himself;
  But should some urgent fate (untimely lot!)
Bring thee to meet his shadow (nameless elf,
  That haunteth the lone regions where hath trod
  No foot of man), commend thyself to God!

EDGAR ALLAN POE

113 To my Mother

Because I feel that, in the Heavens above,
  The Angels, whispering to one another,
Can find, among their burning terms of love,
  None so devotional as that of 'Mother',
Therefore by that dear name I long have called you –
  You who are more than mother unto me,
And fill my heart of hearts, where Death installed you,
  In setting my Virginia's spirit free.
My mother – my own mother, who died early,
  Was but the mother of myself; but you
Are mother to the one I loved so dearly,
  And thus are dearer than the mother I knew
By that infinity with which my wife
Was dearer to my soul than its own soul-life.

EDGAR ALLAN POE

114 **To Science**

Science! True daughter of Old Time thou art!
   Who alterest all things with thy peering eyes.
Why preyest thou thus upon the poet's heart,
   Vulture, whose wings are dull realities?
How should he love thee? or how deem thee wise,
   Who wouldst not leave him in his wandering
To seek for treasure in the jewelled skies,
Albeit he soared with an undaunted wing?
   Hast thou not dragged Diana from her car?
And driven the Hamadryad from the wood
   To seek a shelter in some happier star?
Hast thou not torn the Naiad from her flood,
   The Elfin from the green grass, and from me
   The summer dream beneath the tamarind tree!

EDGAR ALLEN POE

115 From **Bird Parliament**

And as the World upon her victims feeds
So She herself goes down the Way she leads.
   For all her false allurements are the Threads
   The Spider from her Entrail spins, and spreads
For Home and hunting-ground: And by and bye
Darts at due Signal on the tangled Fly,
   Seizes, dis-wings, and drains the Life, and leaves
   The swinging Carcase, and forthwith re-weaves
Her Web: each Victim adding to the store
Of poisoned Entrail to entangle more.
   And so She bloats in Glory: till one Day
   The Master of the House, passing that way,
Perceives, and with one flourish of his Broom
Of Web and Fly and Spider clears the Room.

EDWARD FITZGERALD

116   **The Dead**

I see them, – crowd on crowd they walk the earth,
   Dry leafless trees no autumn wind laid bare;
And in their nakedness find cause for mirth.
   And all unclad would winter's rudeness dare;
No sap doth through their clattering branches flow,
   Whence springing leaves and blossoms bright appear;
Their hearts the living God have ceased to know
   Who gives the spring-time to the expectant year.
They mimic life, as if from Him to steal
   His glow of health to paint the livid cheek;
They borrow words for thoughts they cannot feel,
   That with a seeming heart their tongue may speak;
And in their show of life more dead they live
Than those that to the earth with many tears they give.

                                    JONES VERY

117   **The Sun God**

I saw the Master of the Sun. He stood
   High in his luminous car, himself more bright;
   An Archer of immeasurable might:
On his left shoulder hung his quivered load;
Spurned by his Steeds the eastern mountain glowed;
   Forward his eager eye, and brow of light
He bent; and, while both hands that arch embowed
   Shaft after shaft pursued the flying Night.
No wings profaned that godlike form; around
   His neck high-held an ever-moving crowd
Of locks hung glistening; while such perfect sound
   Fell from his bowstring, that th' ethereal dome
Thrilled as a dewdrop; and each passing cloud
   Expanded, whitening like the ocean foam.

                               AUBREY DE VERE

118 Sorrow

Count each affliction, whether light or grave,
  God's messenger sent down to thee; do thou
  With courtesy receive him; rise and bow;
And, ere his shadow pass thy threshold, crave
Permission first his heavenly feet to lave;
  Then lay before him all thou hast; allow
  No cloud of passion to usurp thy brow,
Or mar thy hospitality; no wave
  Of mortal tumult to obliterate
The soul's marmoreal calmness: Grief should be,
  Like joy, majestic, equable, sedate,
Confirming, cleansing, raising, making free;
  Strong to consume small troubles; to commend
  Great thoughts, grave thoughts, thoughts lasting to the end.

AUBREY DE VERE

119 On Peaceful Death and Painful Life

Why dost thou sorrow for the happy dead?
  For, if their life be lost, their toils are o'er,
  And woe and want can trouble them no more;
Nor ever slept they in an earthly bed
So sound as now they sleep, while dreamless laid
  In the dark chambers of the unknown shore,
  Where Night and Silence guard each sealed door.
So, turn from such as these thy drooping head,
  And mourn the *Dead Alive* – whose spirit flies –
Whose life departs, before his death has come;
  Who knows no Heaven beneath Life's gloomy skies,
Who sees no Hope to brighten up that gloom, –
  'Tis He who feels the worm that never dies, –
The *real* death and darkness of the tomb.

BRANWELL BRONTË

120   Brother and Sister (1)

I cannot choose but think upon the time
   When our two lives grew like two buds that kiss
At lightest thrill from the bee's swinging chime,
   Because the one so near the other is.
He was the elder and a little man
   Of forty inches, bound to show no dread,
And I the girl that puppy-like now ran,
   Now lagged behind my brother's larger tread.
I held him wise, and when he talked to me
   Of snakes and birds, and which God loved the best,
I thought his knowledge marked the boundary
   Where men grew blind, though angels knew the rest.
If he said 'Hush!' I tried to hold my breath;
Wherever he said 'Come!' I stepped in faith.

GEORGE ELIOT

121   Brother and Sister (2)

Long years have left their writing on my brow,
   But yet the freshness and the dew-fed beam
Of those young mornings are about me now,
   When we two wandered toward the far-off stream
With rod and line. Our basket held a store
   Baked for us only, and I thought with joy
That I should have my share, though he had more,
   Because he was the elder and a boy.
The firmaments of daisies since to me
   Have had those mornings in their opening eyes,
The bunchèd cowslip's pale transparency
   Carries that sunshine of sweet memories,
And wild-rose branches take their finest scent
From those blest hours of infantine content.

GEORGE ELIOT

122   Misgivings

When ocean-clouds over inland hills
   Sweep storming in late autumn brown,
And horror the sodden valley fills,
   And the spire falls crashing in the town,
I muse upon my country's ills –
   The tempest bursting from the waste of Time
   On the world's fairest hope linked with man's foulest crime.
Nature's dark side is heeded now –
   (Ah! optimist-cheer disheartened flown)
A child may read the moody brow
   Of yon black mountain lone.
   With shouts the torrents down the gorges go,
And storms are formed behind the storm we feel:
The hemlock shakes in the rafter, the oak in the driving keel.

HERMAN MELVILLE

123   Austerity of Poetry

That son of Italy who tried to blow,
   Ere Dante came, the trump of sacred song,
   In his light youth amid a festal throng
Sate with his bride to see a public show.
Fair was the bride, and on her front did glow
   Youth like a star, and what to youth belong –
   Gay raiment, sparkling gauds, elation strong.
A prop gave way! crash fell a platform! lo,
   'Mid struggling sufferers, hurt to death, she lay!
Shuddering, they drew her garments off – and found
   A robe of sackcloth next the smooth, white skin.
Such, poets, is your bride, the Muse! young, gay,
   Radiant, adorned outside; a hidden ground
Of thought and of austerity within.

MATTHEW ARNOLD

124 East London

'Twas August, and the fierce sun overhead
   Smote on the squalid streets of Bethnal Green,
   And the pale weaver, through his windows seen
In Spitalfields, looked thrice dispirited.
I met a preacher there I knew, and said:
   'Ill and o'erworked, how fare you in this scene?'
   'Bravely!' said he, 'for I of late have been
Much cheered with thoughts of Christ, *the living bread.*'
   O human soul! as long as thou canst so
Set up a mark of everlasting light,
   Above the howling senses' ebb and flow,
To cheer thee, and to right thee if thou roam –
   Not with lost toil thou labourest through the night!
Thou mak'st the heaven thou hop'st indeed thy home.

MATTHEW ARNOLD

125 The Good Shepherd with the Kid

He saves the sheep, the goats he doth not save.
   So rang Tertullian's sentence, on the side
   Of that unpitying Phrygian sect which cried:
'Him can no fount of fresh forgiveness lave,
Who sins, once washed by the baptismal wave.' –
   So spake the fierce Tertullian. But she sighed,
   The infant Church: of love she felt the tide
Stream on her from her Lord's yet recent grave.
   And then she smiled; and in the Catacombs,
With eye suffused but heart inspired true,
   On those walls subterranean, where she hid
Her head 'mid ignominy, death, and tombs,
   She her Good Shepherd's hasty image drew –
And on his shoulders, not a lamb, a kid.

MATTHEW ARNOLD

126   Quiet work

One lesson, Nature, let me learn of thee,
   One lesson which in every wind is blown,
   One lesson of two duties kept at one
Though the loud world proclaim their enmity –
Of toil unsevered from tranquillity!
   Of labour, that in lasting fruit outgrows
   Far noisier schemes, accomplished in repose,
Too great for haste, too high for rivalry!
   Yes, while on earth a thousand discords ring,
Man's senseless uproar mingling with his toil,
   Still do thy quiet ministers move on,
Their glorious tasks in silence perfecting;
   Still working, blaming still our vain turmoil;
Labourers that shall not fail, when man is gone.

MATTHEW ARNOLD

127   Shakespeare

Others abide our question. Thou art free.
   We ask and ask – Thou smilest and art still,
   Out-topping knowledge. For the loftiest hill,
Who to the stars uncrowns his majesty,
Planting his steadfast footsteps in the sea,
   Making the heaven of heavens his dwelling-place,
   Spares but the cloudy border of his base
To the foiled searching of mortality;
   And thou, who didst the stars and sunbeams know,
Self-schooled, self-scanned, self-honoured, self-secure,
   Didst tread on earth unguessed at. – Better so!
All pains the immortal spirit must endure,
   All weakness which impairs, all griefs which bow,
   Find their sole speech in that victorious brow.

MATTHEW ARNOLD

128   **Lucifer in Starlight**

On a starred night Prince Lucifer uprose.
  Tired of his dark dominion swung the fiend
  Above the rolling ball in cloud part screened,
Where sinners hugged their spectre of repose.
Poor prey to his hot fit of pride were those.
  And now upon his western wing he leaned,
  Now his huge bulk o'er Afric's sands careened,
Now the black planet shadowed Arctic snows.
  Soaring through wider zones that pricked his scars
With memory of the old revolt from Awe,
  He reached a middle height, and at the stars,
Which are the brain of heaven, he looked, and sank.
Around the ancient track marched, rank on rank,
  The army of unalterable law.

GEORGE MEREDITH

129   **A Sonnet**

A Sonnet is a moment's monument, –
  Memorial from the Soul's eternity
  To one dead deathless hour. Look that it be,
Whether for lustral rite or dire portent,
Of its own arduous fullness reverent:
  Carve it in ivory or in ebony,
  As Day or Night may rule; and let Time see
Its flowering crest impearled and orient.
  A Sonnet is a coin: its face reveals
The soul, – its converse, to what Power 'tis due: –
  Whether for tribute to the august appeals
Of Life, or dower in Love's high retinue,
  It serve; or, 'mid the dark wharf's cavernous breath,
  In Charon's palm it pay the toll to Death.

DANTE GABRIEL ROSSETTI

130 John Keats

The weltering London ways where children weep
   And girls whom none call maidens laugh, – strange road
   Miring his outward steps, who inly trode
The bright Castalian brink and Latmos' steep: –
Even such his life's cross-paths; till deathly deep
   He toiled through sands of Lethe; and long pain,
   Weary with labour spurned and love found vain,
In dead Rome's sheltering shadow wrapped his sleep.
   O pang-dowered Poet, whose reverberant lips
   And heart-strung lyre awoke the Moon's eclipse, –
Thou whom the daisies glory in growing o'er, –
   Their fragrance clings around thy name, not writ
   But rumoured in water, while the fame of it
Along Time's flood goes echoing evermore.

DANTE GABRIEL ROSSETTI

131 Czar Alexander II (13 March 1881)

From him did forty million serfs, endowed
   Each with six feet of death-due soil, receive
   Rich freeborn lifelong land, whereon to sheave
Their country's harvest. These today aloud
Demand of Heaven a Father's blood, – sore bowed
   With tears and thrilled with wrath; who, while they grieve,
   On every guilty head would fain achieve
All torment by his edicts disallowed.
   He stayed the knout's red-ravening fangs; and first
Of Russian traitors, his own murderers go
White to the tomb. While he, – laid foully low
   With limbs red-rent, with festering brain which erst
   Willed kingly freedom, – 'gainst the deed accurst
To God bears witness of his people's woe.

DANTE GABRIEL ROSSETTI

132   The Church Porch

Sister, first shake we off the dust we have
  Upon our feet, lest it defile the stones
  Inscriptured, covering their sacred bones
Who lie i' the aisles which keep the names they gave,
Their trust abiding round them in the grave;
  Whom painters paint for visible orisons,
  And to whom sculptors pray in stone and bronze;
Their voices echo still like a spent wave.
  Without here, the church-bells are but a tune,
  And on the carven church-door this hot noon
Lays all its heavy sunshine here without:
  But having entered in, we shall find there
  Silence, and sudden dimness, and deep prayer,
And faces of crowned angels all about.

                                    DANTE GABRIEL ROSSETTI

133   Nuptial Sleep

At length their long kiss severed, with sweet smart:
  And as the last slow sudden drops are shed
  From sparkling eaves when all the storm has fled,
So singly flagged the pulses of each heart.
Their bosoms sundered, with the opening start
  Of married flowers to either side outspread
  From the knit stem; yet still their mouths, burnt red,
Fawned on each other where they lay apart.
  Sleep sank them lower than the tide of dreams,
And their dreams watched them sink, and slid away.
  Slowly their souls swam up again, through gleams
Of watered light and dull drowned waifs of day;
  Till from some wonder of new woods and streams
He woke, and wondered more: for there she lay.

                                    DANTE GABRIEL ROSSETTI

134   The Kiss

What smouldering senses in death's sick delay
   Or seizure of malign vicissitude
   Can rob this body of honour, or denude
This soul of wedding-raiment worn today?
For lo! even now my lady's lips did play
   With these my lips such consonant interlude
   As laurelled Orpheus longed for when he wooed
The half-drawn hungering face with that last lay.
   I was a child beneath her touch, – a man
When breast to breast we clung, even I and she, –
A spirit when her spirit looked through me, –
   A god when all our life-breath met to fan
   Our life-blood, till love's emulous ardours ran,
Fire within fire, desire in deity.

DANTE GABRIEL ROSSETTI

135   Silent Noon

Your hands lie open in the long fresh grass, –
   The finger-points look through like rosy blooms:
   Your eyes smile peace. The pasture gleams and glooms
'Neath billowing skies that scatter and amass.
All round our nest, far as the eye can pass,
   Are golden kingcup-fields with silver edge
   Where the cow-parsley skirts the hawthorn-hedge.
'Tis visible silence, still as the hour-glass.
   Deep in the sun-searched growths the dragon-fly
   Hangs like a blue thread loosened from the sky: –
So this wing'd hour is dropt to us from above.
   Oh! clasp we to our hearts, for deathless dower,
   This close-companioned inarticulate hour
When twofold silence was the song of love.

DANTE GABRIEL ROSSETTI

136   A Superscription

Look in my face; my name is Might-have-been;
   I am also called No-more, Too-late, Farewell;
   Unto thine ear I hold the dead-sea shell
Cast up thy Life's foam-fretted feet between;
Unto thine eyes the glass where that is seen
   Which had Life's form and Love's, but by my spell
   Is now a shaken shadow intolerable,
Of ultimate things unuttered the frail screen.
   Mark me, how still I am! But should there dart
One moment through thy soul the soft surprise
Of that winged Peace which lulls the breath of sighs,
   Then shalt thou see me smile, and turn apart
   Thy visage to mine ambush at thy heart
Sleepless with cold commemorative eyes.

DANTE GABRIEL ROSSETTI

137   The Morrow's Message

'Thou Ghost,' I said, 'and is thy name Today? –
   Yesterday's son, with such an abject brow! –
   And can Tomorrow be more pale than thou?'
While yet I spoke, the silence answered: 'Yea,
Henceforth our issue is all grieved and grey,
   And each beforehand makes such poor avow
   As of old leaves beneath the budding bough
Or night-drift that the sundawn shreds away.'
   Then cried I: 'Mother of many malisons,
O Earth, receive me to thy dusty bed!'
But therewithal the tremulous silence said:
   'Lo! Love yet bids thy lady greet thee once: –
   Yea, twice, – whereby thy life is still the sun's;
And thrice, – whereby the shadow of death is dead.'

DANTE GABRIEL ROSSETTI

138 Body's Beauty

Of Adam's first wife, Lilith, it is told
  (The witch he loved before the gift of Eve),
   That, ere the snake's, her sweet tongue could deceive,
And her enchanted hair was the first gold.
And still she sits, young while the earth is old,
  And, subtly of herself contemplative,
   Draws men to watch the bright web she can weave,
Till heart and body and life are in its hold.
   The rose and poppy are her flowers; for where
Is he not found, O Lilith, whom shed scent
  And soft-shed kisses and soft sleep shall snare?
Lo! as that youth's eyes burned at thine, so went
Thy spell through him, and left his straight neck bent
  And round his heart one strangling golden hair.

DANTE GABRIEL ROSSETTI

139 Remember

Remember me when I am gone away,
  Gone far away into the silent land;
  When you can no more hold me by the hand
Nor I half turn to go yet turning stay.
Remember me when no more day by day
  You tell me of our future that you planned:
  Only remember me; you understand
It will be late to counsel then or pray.
  Yet if you should forget me for a while
And afterwards remember, do not grieve:
For if the darkness and corruption leave
  A vestige of the thoughts that once I had,
Better by far you should forget and smile
  Than that you should remember and be sad.

CHRISTINA ROSSETTI

140   Many in after times will say of you

Many in after times will say of you
  'He loved her' – while of me what will they say?
  Not that I loved you more than just in play,
For fashion's sake as idle women do.
Even let them prate; who know not what we knew
  Of love and parting in exceeding pain,
  Of parting hopeless here to meet again,
Hopeless on earth, and heaven is out of view.
But by my heart of love laid bare to you,
  My love that you can make not void nor vain,
Love that forgoes you but to claim anew
  Beyond this passage of the gate of death,
I charge you at the Judgment make it plain
  My love of you was life and not a breath.

CHRISTINA ROSSETTI

141   After Death

The curtains were half drawn, the floor was swept
  And strewn with rushes; rosemary and may
  Lay thick upon the bed on which I lay,
Where through the lattice ivy-shadows crept.
He leaned above me, thinking that I slept
  And could not hear him; but I heard him say:
  'Poor child, poor child': and as he turned away
Came a deep silence, and I knew he wept.
  He did not touch the shroud, or raise the fold
That hid my face, or take my hand in his,
  Or ruffle the smooth pillows for my head:
  He did not love me living; but once dead
He pitied me; and very sweet it is
  To know he still is warm though I am cold.

CHRISTINA ROSSETTI

142   From Sunset to Star Rise

Go from me, summer friends, and tarry not;
   I am no summer friend, but wintry cold,
   A silly sheep benighted from the fold,
A sluggard with a thorn-choked garden plot.
Take counsel, sever from my lot your lot,
   Dwell in your pleasant places, hoard your gold;
   Lest you with me should shiver on the wold,
Athirst and hungering on a barren spot.
   For I have hedged me with a thorny hedge,
I live alone, I look to die alone:
   Yet sometimes when a wind sighs through the sedge
Ghosts of my buried years and friends come back,
   My heart goes sighing after swallows flown
On sometime summer's unreturning track.

CHRISTINA ROSSETTI

143   Love Lies Bleeding

Love that is dead and buried, yesterday
   Out of his grave rose up before my face;
   No recognition in his look, no trace
Of memory in his eyes dust-dimmed and grey:
While I, remembering, found no word to say,
   But felt my quickened heart leap in its place;
   Caught afterglow thrown back from long set days,
Caught echoes of all music passed away.
   Was this indeed to meet? – I mind me yet
In youth we met when hope and love were quick,
   We parted with hope dead, but love alive:
I mind me how we parted then heart sick,
   Remembering, loving, hopeless, weak to strive: –
Was this to meet? Not so, we have not met.

CHRISTINA ROSSETTI

144   Vanity of Vanities

Ah, woe is me for pleasure that is vain,
  Ah, woe is me for glory that is past,
  Pleasure that bringeth sorrow at the last,
Glory that at the last bringeth no gain!
So saith the sinking heart; and so again
  It shall say till the mighty angel-blast
  Is blown, making the sun and moon aghast,
And showering down the stars like sudden rain.
  And evermore men shall go fearfully,
Bending beneath their weight of heaviness;
  And ancient men shall lie down wearily,
And strong men shall rise up in weariness;
  Yea, even the young shall answer sighingly,
Saying one to another: How vain it is!

CHRISTINA ROSSETTI

145   Summer Dawn

Pray but one prayer for me 'twixt thy closed lips,
  Think but one thought of me up in the stars.
The summer night waneth, the morning light slips
  Faint and grey 'twixt the leaves of aspen, betwixt the
    cloud-bars,
That are patiently waiting there for the dawn:
  Patient and colourless, though Heaven's gold
Waits to float through them along with the sun.
  Far out in the meadows, above the young corn,
The heavy elms wait, and restless and cold
  The uneasy wind rises; the roses are dun;
Through the long twilight they pray for the dawn,
  Round the lone house in the midst of the corn.
  Speak but one word to me over the corn,
  Over the tender, bowed locks of the corn.

WILLIAM MORRIS

146   Love and Sleep

Lying asleep between the strokes of night
   I saw my love lean over my sad bed,
   Pale as the duskiest lily's leaf or head,
Smooth-skinned and dark, with bare throat made to bite,
Too wan for blushing and too warm for white,
   But perfect-coloured without white or red.
   And her lips opened amorously, and said
I wist not what, saving one word – Delight.
   And all her face was honey to my mouth,
And all her body pasture to mine eyes;
   The long lithe arms and hotter hands than fire,
The quivering flanks, hair smelling of the south,
   The bright light feet, the splendid supple thighs
And glittering eyelids of my soul's desire.

ALGERNON CHARLES SWINBURNE

147   Hope and Fear

Beneath the shadow of dawn's aerial cope,
   With eyes enkindled as the sun's own sphere,
   Hope from the front of youth in godlike cheer
Looks Godward, past the shades where blind men grope
Round the dark door that prayers nor dreams can ope,
   And makes for joy the very darkness dear
   That gives her wide wings play; nor dreams that fear
At noon may rise and pierce the heart of hope.
   Then, when the soul leaves off to dream and yearn,
   May truth first purge her eyesight to discern
What once being known leaves time no power to appal;
   Till youth at last, ere yet youth be not, learn
The kind wise word that falls from years that fall –
'Hope thou not much, and fear thou not at all.'

ALGERNON CHARLES SWINBURNE

148 Transfiguration

But half a man's days – and his days were nights.
   What hearts were ours who loved him, should we pray
   That night would yield him back to darkling day,
Sweet death that soothes, to life that spoils and smites?
For now, perchance, life lovelier than the light's
   That shed no comfort on his weary way
   Shows him what none may dream to see or say
Ere yet the soul may scale those topless heights
   Where death lies dead, and triumph. Haply there
Already may his kindling eyesight find
   Faces of friends – no face than his more fair –
And first among them found of all his kind
   Milton, with crowns from Eden on his hair,
And eyes that meet a brother's now not blind.

                    ALGERNON CHARLES SWINBURNE

149 Hermaphroditus (II)

Where between sleep and life some brief space is,
   With love like gold bound round about the head,
   Sex to sweet sex with lips and limbs is wed,
Turning the fruitful feud of hers and his
To the waste wedlock of a sterile kiss;
   Yet from them something like as fire is shed
   That shall not be assuaged till death be dead,
Though neither life nor sleep can find out this.
   Love made himself of flesh that perisheth
A pleasure-house for all the loves his kin;
   But on the one side sat a man like death,
And on the other a woman sat like sin.
   So with veiled eyes and sobs between his breath
Love turned himself and would not enter in.

                    ALGERNON CHARLES SWINBURNE

150   Hermaphroditus (IV)

Yea, love, I see; it is not love but fear.
   Nay, sweet, it is not fear but love, I know;
   Or wherefore should thy body's blossom blow
So sweetly, or thine eyelids leave so clear
Thy gracious eyes that never made a tear –
   Though for their love our tears like blood should flow,
   Though love and life and death should come and go,
So dreadful, so desirable, so dear?
   Yea, sweet, I know; I saw in what swift wise
Beneath the woman's and the water's kiss
Thy moist limbs melted into Salmacis,
   And the large light turned tender in thine eyes,
   And all thy boy's breath softened into sighs;
But Love being blind, how should he know of this?

ALGERNON CHARLES SWINBURNE

151   The Marseillaise

What means this mighty chant, wherein its wail
   Of some intolerable woe, grown strong
   With sense of more intolerable wrong
Swells to a stern victorious march – a gale
Of vengeful wrath? What mean the faces pale,
   The fierce resolve, the ecstatic pangs along
   Life's fiery ways, the demon thoughts which throng
The gates of awe, when these wild notes assail
   The sleeping of our souls? Hear ye no more
Than the mad foam of revolution's leaven,
   Than a roused people's throne-o'erwhelming tread?
Hark! 'tis man's spirit thundering on the shore
   Of iron fate; the tramp of Titans dread,
Sworn to dethrone the Gods unjust from Heaven.

JOHN TODHUNTER

152 Hap

If but some vengeful god would call to me
    From up the sky, and laugh: 'Thou suffering thing,
Know that thy sorrow is my ecstasy,
    That thy love's loss is my hate's profiting!'
Then would I bear it, clench myself, and die,
    Steeled by the sense of ire unmerited;
Half-eased in that a Powerfuller than I
    Had willed and meted me the tears I shed.
But not so. How arrives it joy lies slain,
    And why unblooms the best hope ever sown?
— Crass Casualty obstructs the sun and rain,
    And dicing Time for gladness casts a moan . . .
    These purblind Doomsters had as readily strown
Blisses about my pilgrimage as pain.

THOMAS HARDY

153 A Church Romance

She turned in the high pew, until her sight
    Swept the west gallery, and caught its row
    Of music-men with viol, book, and bow
Against the sinking sad tower-window light.
She turned again; and in her pride's despite
    One strenuous viol's inspirer seemed to throw
    A message from his string to her below,
Which said: 'I claim thee as my own forthright!'
    Thus their hearts' bond began, in due time signed.
And long years thence, when Age had scared Romance,
At some old attitude of his or glance
    That gallery-scene would break upon her mind,
With him as minstrel, ardent, young, and trim,
Bowing 'New Sabbath' or 'Mount Ephraïm'.

THOMAS HARDY

154   In the Cemetery

'You see those mothers squabbling there?'
    Remarks the man of the cemetery.
'One says in tears, '"Tis mine lies here!"
    Another, "Nay, mine, you Pharisee!"
Another, "How dare you move my flowers
And put your own on this grave of ours!"
    But all their children were laid therein
    At different times, like sprats in a tin.
And then the main drain had to cross,
    And we moved the lot some nights ago,
And packed them away in the general foss
    With hundreds more. But their folks don't know,
And as well cry over a new-laid drain
As anything else, to ease your pain!'

THOMAS HARDY

155   She, to Him (1)

When you shall see me in the toils of Time,
    My lauded beauties carried off from me,
My eyes no longer stars as in their prime,
    My name forgot of Maiden Fair and Free;
When, in your being, heart concedes to mind,
    And judgment, though You scarce its process know,
Recalls the excellencies I once enshrined,
    And you are irked that they have withered so:
Remembering mine the loss is, not the blame,
    That Sportsman Time but rears his brood to kill,
Knowing me in my soul the very same –
    One who would die to spare you touch of ill! –
Will you not grant to old affection's claim
    The hand of friendship down Life's sunless hill?

THOMAS HARDY

156 Don Quixote

Behind thy pasteboard, on thy battered hack,
    Thy lean cheek striped with plaster to and fro,
    Thy long spear levelled at the unseen foe,
And doubtful Sancho trudging at thy back,
Thou wert a figure strange enough, good lack!
    To make wiseacredom, both high and low,
    Rub purblind eyes, and (having watched thee go)
Dispatch its Dogberrys upon thy track:
    Alas! poor Knight! Alas! poor soul possessed!
Yet would today, when Courtesy grows chill,
    And life's fine loyalties are turned to jest,
Some fire of thine might burn within us still!
    Ah, would but one might lay his lance in rest
And charge in earnest – were it but a mill!

AUSTIN DOBSON

157 An April Pastoral

He   Whither away, fair Neat-herdess?
She   Shepherd, I go to tend my kine.
He   Stay thou, and watch this flock of mine.
She   With thee? Nay, that were idleness.
He   Thy kine will pasture none the less.
She   Not so: they wait me and my sign.
He   I'll pipe to thee beneath the pine.
She   Thy pipe will soothe not their distress.
He   Dost thou not hear beside the spring
                How the gay birds are carolling?
She   I hear them. But it may not be.
He   Farewell then, Sweetheart! Farewell now.
She   Shepherd, farewell . . . Where goest thou?
He   I go . . . to tend thy kine for thee!

AUSTIN DOBSON

158   Farewell to Juliet

Farewell, then. It is finished. I forgo
  With this all right in you, even that of tears.
If I have spoken hardly, it will show
  How much I loved you. With you disappears
  A glory, a romance of many years.
What you may be henceforth I will not know.
  The phantom of your presence on my fears
Is impotent at length for weal or woe.
  Your past, your present, all alike must fade
In a new land of dreams, where love is not.
  Then kiss me and farewell. The choice is made,
And we shall live to see the past forgot,
    If not forgiven. See, I came to curse,
    Yet stay to bless. I know not which is worse.

WILFRID SCAWEN BLUNT

159   On the Shortness of Time

If I could live without the thought of Death,
  Forgetful of Time's waste, the soul's decay,
I would not ask for other joy than breath
  With light and sound of birds and the sun's ray.
  I could sit on untroubled day by day
Watching the grass grow, and the wild flowers range
  From blue to yellow and from red to grey
In natural sequence as the seasons change.
  I could afford to wait, but for the hurt
Of this dull tick of time which chides my ear.
  But now I dare not sit with loins ungirt
And staff unlifted, for Death stands too near.
    I must be up and doing – ay, each minute.
    The grave gives time for rest when we are in it.

WILFRID SCAWEN BLUNT

160   The Oasis of Sidi Khaled

How the earth burns! Each pebble underfoot
　Is as a living thing with power to wound.
The white sand quivers, and the footfall mute
　Of the slow camels strikes but gives no sound,
　As though they walked on flame, not solid ground.
'Tis noon, and the beasts' shadows even have fled
　Back to their feet, and there is fire around
And fire beneath, and overhead the sun.
　Pitiful heaven! What is this we view?
Tall trees, a river, pools, where swallows fly,
　Thickets of oleander where doves coo,
Shades, deep as midnight, greenness for tired eyes.
　Hark, how the light winds in the palm-tops sigh.
Oh this is rest. Oh this is paradise.

WILFRID SCAWEN BLUNT

161   Musing on Venice and the thought of thee

Musing on Venice and the thought of thee,
　Thou resolute angel, sleep o'erspread my brain;
　Brief solace blossomed from the root of pain,
For in my dream thou wert at one with me:
No longer restless like that clear blue sea,
　No longer lost in schemes of sordid gain,
　No longer unattainable by strain
Of futile arms and false love's mockery;
　But tranquil, with thy large eyes fixed on mine;
Love's dove-wings moving on thy soul's abyss;
　Thy lips half-opened, and thy breast divine
Scarce heaving with an unacknowledged bliss;
　And all the golden glory that is thine,
Communicated in a long close kiss.

JOHN ADDINGTON SYMONDS

162   When We Are All Asleep

When He returns, and finds the World so drear –
   All sleeping, – young and old, unfair and fair,
Will He stoop down and whisper in each ear,
   'Awaken!' or for pity's sake forbear, –
   Saying, 'How shall I meet their frozen stare
Of wonder, and their eyes so full of fear?
   How shall I comfort them in their despair,
If they cry out, "Too late! let us sleep here"?'
   Perchance He will not wake us up, but when
He sees us look so happy in our rest,
   Will murmur, 'Poor dead women and dead men!
Dire was their doom, and weary was their quest.
   Wherefore awake them unto life again?
Let them sleep on untroubled – it is best.'

ROBERT BUCHANAN

163   The End of the Æon

The end of the old order draweth nigh;
   The air is thick with signs of coming change;
   Forebodings vague through all men's fancies range,
Dim clouds of doubt, that overcast the sky,
And mists of fear, that darken every eye.
   In hut and hall, in town and tower and grange,
   Men's souls are sick with visions void and strange,
Delirious dreams of those about to die.
   No faith there is but is a phantom grown
Of its old self; the Gods by doubt and Fate
   Are frozen back to shapes of senseless stone.
All eyes are fixed upon the Future's gate,
For that which is to be, and all things wait
   To hail the coming of the Gods unknown.

JOHN PAYNE

164   The Singer

'That was the thrush's last good-night,' I thought,
   And heard the soft descent of summer rain
   In the drooped garden leaves; but hush! again
The perfect iterence, – freer than unsought
   Odours of violets dim in woodland ways,
Deeper than coiled waters laid a-dream
Below mossed ledges of a shadowy stream,
   And faultless as blown roses in June days.
Full-throated singer! art thou thus anew
   Voiceful to hear how round thyself alone
The enriched silence drops for thy delight
   More soft than snow, more sweet than honeydew?
Now cease: the last faint western streak is gone,
   Stir not the blissful quiet of the night.

EDWARD DOWDEN

165   Felix Randal

Felix Randal the farrier, O he is dead then? My duty all ended,
  Who have watched his mould of man, big-boned and hardy-
      handsome
  Pining, pining, till time when reason rambled in it and some
Fatal four disorders, fleshed there, all contended?

Sickness broke him. Impatient he cursed at first, but mended
  Being anointed and all; though a heavenlier heart began some
  Months earlier, since I had our sweet reprieve and ransom
Tendered to him. Ah well, God rest him all road ever he offended!

  This seeing the sick endears them to us, us too it endears.
  My tongue had taught thee comfort, touch had quenched thy
      tears,
Thy tears that touched my heart, child, Felix, poor Felix Randal;

  How far from then forethought of, all thy more boisterous
      years,
  When thou at the random grim forge, powerful amidst peers,
Didst fettle for the great grey drayhorse his bright and battering
    sandal!

GERARD MANLEY HOPKINS

166 Renouncement

I must not think of thee; and, tired yet strong,
   I shun the thought that lurks in all delight –
   The thought of thee – and in the blue Heaven's height,
And in the sweetest passage of a song.
O just beyond the fairest thoughts that throng
   This breast, the thought of thee waits hidden yet bright;
   But it must never, never come in sight;
I must stop short of thee the whole day long.
   But when sleep comes to close each difficult day,
When night gives pause to the long watch I keep
   And all my bonds I needs must loose apart,
Must doff my will as raiment laid away, –
   With the first dream that comes with the first sleep
I run, I run, I am gathered to thy heart.

ALICE MEYNELL

167 Your own fair youth

Your own fair youth, you care so little for it,
   Smiling towards Heaven you would not stay the advances
   Of time and change upon your happiest fancies.
I keep your golden hour, and will restore it.
If ever, in time to come, you would explore it –
   Your old self, whose thoughts went like last year's pansies,
   Look unto me; no mirror keeps its glances;
In my unfailing praises now I store it.
   To guard all joys of yours from Time's estranging,
I shall be then a treasury where your gay,
   Happy, and pensive past unaltered is.
I shall be then a garden charmed from changing,
   In which your June has never passed away.
Walk there awhile among my memories.

ALICE MEYNELL

168   On hearing the *Dies Irae* sung in the Sistine Chapel

Nay, Lord, not thus! White lilies in the spring,
  Sad olive-groves, or silver-breasted dove,
  Teach me more clearly of Thy life and love
Than terrors of red flame and thundering.
The hillside vines dear memories of Thee bring:
  A bird at evening flying to its nest
  Tells me of One who had no place of rest:
I think it is of Thee the sparrows sing.
  Come rather on some autumn afternoon,
When red and brown are burnished on the leaves,
  And the fields echo to the gleaner's song,
Come when the splendid fullness of the moon,
  Looks down upon the rows of golden sheaves,
And reap Thy harvest: we have waited long.

OSCAR WILDE

169   On the Sale by Auction of Keats' Love Letters

These are the letters which Endymion wrote
  To one he loved in secret, and apart.
  And now the brawlers of the auction mart
Bargain and bid for each poor blotted note,
Ay! for each separate pulse of passion quote
  The merchant's price. I think they love not art
  Who break the crystal of a poet's heart
That small and sickly eyes may glare and gloat.
  Is it not said that many years ago,
In a far Eastern town, some soldiers ran
With torches through the midnight, and began
  To wrangle for mean raiment, and to throw
Dice for the garments of a wretched man,
  Not knowing the God's wonder, or His woe?

OSCAR WILDE

170 *Hélas!*

To drift with every passion till my soul
  Is a stringed lute on which all winds can play,
  Is it for this that I have given away
Mine ancient wisdom, and austere control?
Methinks my life is a twice-written scroll
  Scrawled over on some boyish holiday
  With idle songs for pipe and virelay,
Which do but mar the secret of the whole.
  Surely there was a time I might have trod
The sunlit heights, and from life's dissonance
  Struck one clear chord to reach the ears of God:
  Is that time dead? Lo! with a little rod
I did but touch the honey of romance –
And must I lose a soul's inheritance?

OSCAR WILDE

171 In Hospital

Under the shadow of a hawthorn brake,
  Where bluebells draw the sky down to the wood,
Where, 'mid brown leaves, the primroses awake
  And hidden violets smell of solitude;
Beneath green leaves bright-fluttered by the wing
Of fleeting, beautiful, immortal Spring,
  I should have said, 'I love you,' and your eyes
  Have said, 'I, too . . .' The gods saw otherwise.
For this is winter, and the London streets
  Are full of soldiers from that far, fierce fray
Where life knows death, and where poor glory meets
  Full-face with shame, and weeps and turns away.
And in the broken, trampled foreign wood
Is horror, and the terrible scent of blood,
  And love shines tremulous, like a drowning star,
  Under the shadow of the wings of war.

E. NESBIT

172   On Wordsworth

Two voices are there: one is of the deep;
   It learns the storm-cloud's thunderous melody,
   Now roars, now murmurs with the changing sea,
Now bird-like pipes, now closes soft in sleep,
And one is of an old half-witted sheep
   Which bleats articulate monotony,
   And indicates that two and one are three,
That grass is green, lakes damp, and mountains steep:
   And, Wordsworth, both are thine: at certain times
   Forth from the heart of thy melodious rhymes
The form and pressure of high thoughts will burst:
   At other times – good Lord! I'd rather be
   Quite unacquainted with the A B C
Than write such hopeless rubbish as thy worst.

JAMES KENNETH STEPHEN

173   First and Last Kiss

Thy lips are quiet, and thine eyes are still;
   Cold, colourless, and sad thy placid face;
   Thy form has only now the statue's grace;
My words wake not thy voice, nor can they fill
Thine eyes with light. Before fate's mighty will,
   Our wills must bow; yet for a little space,
   I sit with thee and death, in this lone place,
And hold thy hands that are so white and chill.
   I always loved thee, though thou didst not know;
But well he knew whose wedded love thou wert:
   Now thou art dead, I may raise up the fold
That hides thy face, and, o'er thee bending low,
   For the first time and last before we part,
Kiss the curved lips – calm, beautiful, and cold!

PHILIP BOURKE MARSTON

174   My Life

To me my life seems as a haunted house,
   The ways and passages whereof are dumb;
   Up whose decaying stair no footsteps come;
Lo, this the hall hung with sere laurel boughs,
Where long years back came victors to carouse.
   But none of all that company went home;
   For scarce their lips had quaffed the bright wine's foam,
When sudden Death brake dank upon their brows.
   Here in this lonely, ruined house I dwell,
   While unseen fingers toll the chapel bell;
Sometimes the arras rustles, and I see
   A half-veiled figure through the twilight steal,
Which, when I follow, pauses suddenly
   Before the door whereon is set a seal.

PHILIP BOURKE MARSTON

175   In the Cloisters, Winchester College

I walked today where Past and Present meet,
   In that grey cloister eloquent of years,
   Which ever groweth old, yet ever hears
The same glad echo of unaging feet.
Only from brass and stone some quaint conceit,
   The monument of long-forgotten tears,
   Whispers of vanished lives, of spent careers,
And hearts that, beating once, have ceased to beat.
   And as I walked, I heard the boys who played
Beyond the quiet precinct, and I said –
   'How broad the gulf which delving Time has made
Between those happy living and these dead.'
And, lo, I spied a grave new-garlanded,
   And on the wall a boyish face that prayed.

EDWARD CRACROFT LEFROY

176   A Cricket Bowler

Two minutes' rest till the next man goes in!
   The tired arms lie with every sinew slack
   On the mown grass. Unbent the supple back,
And elbows apt to make the leather spin
Up the slow bat and round the unwary shin, –
   In knavish hands a most unkindly knack;
   But no guile shelters under this boy's black
Crisp hair, frank eyes, and honest English skin.
   Two minutes only. Conscious of a name,
The new man plants his weapon with profound
   Long-practised skill that no mere trick may scare.
Not loth, the rested lad resumes the game:
   The flung ball takes one madding tortuous bound,
And the mid-stump three somersaults in air.

EDWARD CRACROFT LEFROY

177   As in the midst of battle

As in the midst of battle there is room
   For thoughts of love, and in foul sin for mirth;
   As gossips whisper of a trinket's worth
Spied by the death-bed's flickering candle-gloom;
As in the crevices of Caesar's tomb
   The sweet herbs flourish on a little earth:
   So in this great disaster of our birth
We can be happy, and forget our doom.
   For morning, with a ray of tenderest joy
Gilding the iron heaven, hides the truth,
   And evening gently woos us to employ
Our grief in idle catches. Such is youth;
   Till from that summer's trance we wake, to find
   Despair before us, vanity behind.

GEORGE SANTAYANA

178   Leda and the Swan

A sudden blow: the great wings beating still
   Above the staggering girl, her thighs caressed
By the dark webs, her nape caught in his bill,
   He holds her helpless breast upon his breast.
How can those terrified vague fingers push
   The feathered glory from her loosening thighs?
And how can body, laid in that white rush,
   But feel the strange heart beating where it lies?
A shudder in the loins engenders there
   The broken wall, the burning roof and tower
And Agamemnon dead. Being so caught up,
   So mastered by the brute blood of the air,
Did she put on his knowledge with his power
   Before the indifferent beak could let her drop?

WILLIAM BUTLER YEATS

179   Let us leave talking of angelic hosts

Let us leave talking of angelic hosts,
   Of nebulae, and lunar hemispheres,
   And what the days, and what the Uranian years
Shall offer us when you and I are ghosts;
Forget the festivals and pentecosts
   Of metaphysics, and the lesser fears
   Confound us, and seal up our eyes and ears
Like little rivers locked below the frosts.
   And let us creep into the smallest room
That any hunted exile has desired
For him and for his love when he was tired;
   And sleep oblivious of any doom
Which is beyond our reason to conceive;
And so forget to weep, forget to grieve,
   And wake, and touch each other's hands, and turn
   Upon a bed of juniper and fern.

ELINOR WYLIE

180   The Soldier

If I should die, think only this of me:
   That there's some corner of a foreign field
That is for ever England. There shall be
   In that rich earth a richer dust concealed;
A dust whom England bore, shaped, made aware,
   Gave, once, her flowers to love, her ways to roam,
A body of England's, breathing English air,
   Washed by the rivers, blest by suns of home.
And think, this heart, all evil shed away,
   A pulse in the eternal mind, no less
Gives somewhere back the thoughts by England given;
   Her sights and sounds; dreams happy as her day;
And laughter, learnt of friends; and gentleness,
   In hearts at peace, under an English heaven.

RUPERT BROOKE

181   The Busy Heart

Now that we've done our best and worst, and parted,
   I would fill my mind with thoughts that will not rend
(O heart, I do not dare go empty-hearted)
   I'll think of Love in books, Love without end;
Women with child, content; and old men sleeping;
   And wet strong ploughlands, scarred for certain grain;
And babes that weep, and so forget their weeping;
   And the young heavens, forgetful after rain;
And evening hush, broken by homing wings;
   And Song's nobility, and Wisdom holy,
That live, we dead. I would think of a thousand things,
   Lovely and durable, and taste them slowly,
One after one, like tasting a sweet food.
I have need to busy my heart with quietude.

RUPERT BROOKE

182 One Day

Today I have been happy. All the day
   I held the memory of you, and wove
Its laughter with the dancing light o' the spray,
   And sowed the sky with tiny clouds of love,
And sent you following the white waves of sea,
   And crowned your head with fancies, nothing worth,
Stray buds from that old dust of misery,
   Being glad with a new foolish quiet mirth.
So lightly I played with those dark memories,
Just as a child, beneath the summer skies,
   Plays hour by hour with a strange shining stone,
For which (he knows not) towns were fire of old,
   And love has been betrayed, and murder done,
And great kings turned to a little bitter mould.

RUPERT BROOKE

183 Sonnet Reversed

Hand trembling towards hand; the amazing lights
Of heart and eye. They stood on supreme heights.

   Ah, the delirious weeks of honeymoon!
Soon they returned, and, after strange adventures,
   Settled at Balham by the end of June.
Their money was in Can. Pacs. B. Debentures,
   And in Antofagastas. Still he went
Cityward daily; still she did abide
   At home. And both were really quite content
With work and social pleasures. Then they died.
   They left three children (besides George, who drank):
The eldest, Jane, who married Mr Bell,
   William, the head-clerk in the County Bank,
And Henry, a stockbroker, doing well.

RUPERT BROOKE

184 On Somme

Suddenly into the still air burst thudding
  And thudding, and cold fear possessed me all,
On the grey slopes there, where winter in sullen brooding
  Hung between height and depth of the ugly fall
Of Heaven to earth; and the thudding was illness' own.
  But still a hope I kept that were we there going over,
  I in the line, I should not fail, but take recover
From others' courage, and not as coward be known.
No flame we saw, the noise and the dread alone
  Was battle to us; men were enduring there such
And such things, in wire tangled, to shatters blown.
  Courage kept, but ready to vanish at first touch.
Fear, but just held. Poets were luckier once
In the hot fray swallowed and some magnificence.

IVOR GURNEY

185 How Do I Love Thee?

I cannot woo thee as the lion his mate,
  With proud parade and fierce prestige of presence;
Nor thy fleet fancy may I captivate
  With pastoral attitudes in flowery pleasance;
Nor will I kneeling court thee with sedate
  And comfortable plans of husbandhood;
Nor file before thee as a candidate . . .
  I cannot woo thee as a lover would.
To wrest thy hand from rivals, iron-gloved,
  Or cheat them by a craft, I am not clever.
But I do love thee even as Shakespeare loved,
  Most gently wild, and desperately for ever,
Full-hearted, grave, and manfully in vain,
With thought, high pain, and ever vaster pain.

WILFRED OWEN

186   'next to of course god america i'

'next to of course god america i
   love you land of the pilgrims' and so forth oh
say can you see by the dawn's early my
   country 'tis of centuries come and go
and are no more what of it we should worry
   in every language even deafanddumb
thy sons acclaim your glorious name by gorry
   by jingo by gee by gosh by gum
why talk of beauty what could be more beaut-
   iful than these heroic happy dead
who rushed like lions to the roaring slaughter
   they did not stop to think they died instead
then shall the voice of liberty be mute?'

He spoke. And drank rapidly a glass of water

E. E. CUMMINGS

187   Lines Written on a Seat on the Grand Canal, Dublin, 'Erected to the Memory of Mrs Dermot O'Brien'

O commemorate me where there is water,
   Canal water preferably, so stilly
Greeny at the heart of summer. Brother
   Commemorate me thus beautifully
Where by a lock niagarously roars
   The falls for those who sit in the tremendous silence
Of mid-July. No one will speak in prose
   Who finds his way to these Parnassian islands.
A swan goes by head low with many apologies,
   Fantastic light looks through the eyes of bridges –
And look! a barge comes bringing from Athy
   And other far-flung towns mythologies.
O commemorate me with no hero-courageous
   Tomb – just a canal-bank seat for the passer-by.

PATRICK KAVANAGH

188   Vicarious

Increasingly, our joys become vicarious;
    Watching a daughter's face light up with wonder
On swings or roundabouts, or turn hilarious
    At a crazy rhyme or a linguistic blunder,
We come to require unseasonable devices;
    Can't pass a funfair; revel in the ferment
Of Brighton beach or in the queue for ices
    Or games which till not long ago were torment.
Vicarious, too, our troubles: we detest
    The rain which spoils hopscotch or rounders; mourn
The loss of a doll, death of a fish. The best
    Part of us comes away and is reborn.
And if a child runs off, in the dark frost
We find it is ourselves that we have lost.

EDWARD LOWBURY

189   Air-Raid Warning
(A Monosyllabic Sonnet)

Though
    Night
    Fright
Grow,
No
    Bright
    Light
Show!
    This
Law
    Is
For
    You
    Too!

NOEL PETTY

190   No More Access to Her Underpants

Her red dress stretched across the remembered small
of her dear bare back, bare for me no more,
   that once so nicely bent itself in bed
   to take my thrusts and then my stunned caress,
disclosing to my sated gaze a film
of down, of sheen, upon the dulcet skin –
   her red dress stretched, I say, as carapace
   upon her tasty flesh, she shows a face
of stone and turns to others at the party.
   Her ass, its solemn cleft; her breasts, their tips
as tender in colour as the milk-white bit
   above the pubic curls; her eyes like pits
of warmth in the tousled light: all forfeit,
   and locked in antarctic ice by this bitch.

JOHN UPDIKE

191   'Scorn not the sonnet' (Wordsworth)

Scorn not the sonnet on the sonnet, critic;
   It is a bank where poets love to lie
   And praise each other's ingenuity
In finding such a form. The analytic
Reader may stigmatise as parasitic
   The mirror-image of a mystery,
   This echo of lost voices, find it dry,
And intellectually paralytic.
   Yet 'tis a child of Fancy, light and live,
A fragile veil of Nature, scarcely worn
   (Of Wordsworth's two, of Shakespeare's none, survive);
Empty not then the vials of scorn upon it.
   Nor, since we're on the subject, should you scorn
The sonnet on the sonnet on the sonnet.

PETER DICKINSON

Notes

Figures in italic indicate sonnet numbers

1 An Italian sonnet, which happens to have a terminal couplet. The rhyme-scheme is *abba abba cddc ee*.

3 An English sonnet, clearly defined as such by the offsetting of each quatrain through anaphora (identity of line-beginning), 'Set me . . .', and the further offsetting of the terminal couplet. The rhyme-scheme is *abab cdcd efef gg*.

4 A good example of a Spenserian stanza, rhyming *abab bcbc cdcd ee*.

19 An unusual example of multiple anaphora, ten of the fourteen lines beginning with 'And . . .' This should not be thought of as negligent technique. Shakespeare uses a deliberately tedious method in order to indicate the wearisome, repetitive round of wickedness and disappointment in the world, from which only love can rescue him.

23 As indicated in the Introduction, this sonnet reads like a parody of no. 13.

24 Here Shakespeare experiments with a shorter line, a tetrameter, sacrificing the asymmetry of the pentameter. (See Introduction.) The attempt is not particularly successful and has had very few imitators.

25 Shakespeare often interpolates a few rhymes into the (unrhymed) Blank Verse of his plays, sometimes to mark the ending of a scene or act. It is rare for him to insinuate an entire sonnet. He chooses to do this in *Romeo and Juliet* at a particularly poignant moment, in Act I, scene v, when the two young lovers meet for the first time. Romeo has already seen Juliet from afar and fallen in love with her at first sight. Perhaps this is the moment when Juliet falls in love with Romeo. It is certainly the beginning of the real action of the play. There are two other sonnets in this play, but, whereas this one is hidden away in the text, the others are exposed for performance by a Chorus.

34 This famous sonnet is a good example of the Miltonic form. Note the powerful enjambement which carries the sense over from line 8 to line 9, 'But Patience, to prevent / That murmur, soon replies . . .' This is an emphatic rejection of the need for a clear break between octave and sestet. In other respects the sonnet is Italianate, with the rhyme-scheme: *abba abba cde cde*.

35 Another Miltonic sonnet with strong enjambement between lines 8 and 9, this is an early example of the broadening of subject matter for use in sonnet form. Although religious in tone, the sonnet is political in meaning. Milton makes clear his support for the Italians against the Piedmontese.

37 This is an Italian sonnet with an unusual rhyme-scheme: *aabbccdd eefggf*. This form, which puts twelve of the fourteen lines into couplets, was used on a number of occasions by Ayres.

39 A rare early example of a sonnet written entirely in couplets. Another example in Ayres' work may be seen in 'The Scholar of His Own Pupil'.

40 Rochester wrote no sonnets as such, but at least two of his lyrics have a strong appearance of sonnet-like structure. 'Régime de Vivre', although written in couplets, devotes eight lines to sex with the poet's mistress and six to sex with his page. 'Sonnet' 40, also sexual in content, has an appropriate break, marked by a full-stop, at the end of line 8. The rollicking tone of this poem, well-suited to its licentious spirit, derives from the use of an unusual metre. Technically speaking these are anapaestic lines with many variations. An anapaest is a foot of three syllables of which the third one is stressed, as in the phrase 'tally-hó!' Many of the unstressed syllables are (legitimately) omitted; four perfect anapaestic tetrameters (te-te-túm, te-te-túm, te-te-túm, te-te-túm) are visible in lines 3, 5, 10 and 13. The poet's offer of 'a galloping notion' in line 2 is explained by his choice of this galloping measure.

53 The opening line repeats that of sonnet 9 by Sir Philip Sidney.

56 The addressee is Mrs Sarah Siddons (1755–1831), the leading tragic actress for three decades (1782–1812), renowned for her portrayal of Lady Macbeth.

57 This is an inversion of the Italian sonnet in which curious rhyming (supported by the punctuation) places the sestet before the octave: *ababbb ccddeeff*.

60 This poem parodies the art of sonneteering and satirises feeble poets who use the form. To drive the joke home, Elliott uses feminine (two-syllable rhymes) throughout the first twelve lines, which cannot be done in English without creating a comic effect. (See the four rhymes: daughter/caught her/water/slaughter.) He signs off with a flourish by reverting to masculine rhymes for his final couplet. Cf. 107, in which Tennyson goes one better, using feminine rhymes throughout.

61 Here is some splendid rhyming with proper names, to good comic effect. In speaking of his various Johns, Elliot manages to rhyme that plural word with 'offs and ons', only to surpass this by squeezing a rhyme between the surnames of two of his named subjects: Knox/Locke's.

70 Unusual rhyming gives this celebrated sonnet a flavour of its own: *ababacdcede-fef*. This is neither Italian nor English; neither Spenserian nor Miltonic. The opening and closing quatrains give the stanza a spurious air of normality, but its middle section is chaotic. Stretching a point we can allow 'appear' to rhyme with both 'despair' and 'bare', which brings these inner lines into something like unity. The meaning provides the expected clear break after line 8, but the harking back of 'kings' at the end of line 10 to rhyme with line 7 reunites the sestet with octave. No two successive lines rhyme together, and there is one run of four successive lines which do not rhyme together ('frown', 'command', 'read', 'things', at the ends of lines 4–7).

74 Another sonnet with unusual and complex rhyming. The scheme goes as follows: *abababccadcdcc* – a strange mixture indeed. In order to arrive at even this degree of rhyme we have to allow two examples of approximate rhyming: 'path' with 'death' (lines 10 and 12) and 'you' (line 13) with 'go', 'know', 'woe' and 'below' (lines 7, 8, 11 and 14). Without this neither would have a rhyming partner. But the result is that there are *five* rhymes linking lines 7, 8, 11, 13 and 14, which is virtually unheard of in sonnet-rhyming, as would be any odd number of rhymes. Taking 70 and 74 together we can hand to Shelley the palm for inventiveness in rhyming patterns. This is an excellent way to take advantage of the sonnet form without running the risk of formal repetitiveness.

75 One of several sonnets written by Clare as sonnets, but in couplets. (See also 39, 76, 115.)

76 See 75.

86 **rathe** (or ruth): archaism for quick or eager, or in this context, early.

89 A reversion to the Spenserian sonnet form, interesting because of its rarity.

91 An early example of an unrhymed sonnet, also lacking one foot in the first

line, which is a tetrameter. These irregularities are paid for in full by the magnificence of the poetic language of this poem. Phrases like 'river dragon', 'snowy trochilus' and the splendid 'brown habergeon of his limbs enamelled / With sanguine alamandines . . .' would be outrageous in another context, but here they form a glove-like fit with the exotic subject. How better could anyone describe a crocodile?

92 The six rhymes used in this sonnet have an unusual arrangement: *abbacdcedefeff.*

99 The last line of this sonnet is lengthened by an extra foot, making it a hexameter. Let us give credit for inventiveness to the poet; this is likely to be deliberate. Tennyson did the same thing in his 'Kraken' sonnet (103), as did Jones Very in 'The Dead' (116). By this unusual device all three poems achieve a true sense of grandeur just where it is required.

103 See 99.

107 This awful poetry reads like a computer-assisted translation from the Russian. The use of feminine (two-syllable) rhymes throughout is, thank goodness, rare, perhaps unique. Mountain and fountain, having been rhymed in 'Good King Wenceslas', can never again be strikingly paired. Six out of seven successive lines end in '-ing'. Line 12 is one of the worst in English poetry.

110 **Bucephalus** (meaning 'bull-headed') was an uncontrollable horse shown to Alexander the Great by his father. Noticing that the steed was afraid of his own shadow, Alexander turned him towards the sun and then mounted him with ease.

112 This sonnet is a gate-crasher in disguise. It looks plausible enough, seeming to have a run of quatrains followed by a terminal couplet – just what Shakespeare did, except that one of the quatrains is *abba* (envelope) rather than *abab* (alternating). But there is one further difference. Somehow the poet has sneaked in an extra line. When line 8 ends we should be off into the final sestet, but instead of that the anomalous line 9 repeats a rhyme which has already completed itself, by adding 'more' to the previous 'lore' and 'shore' (5, 8). Add up the lines and you will get to fifteen.

115 This piece, although not conceived as such by its author, has all the qualities of a good sonnet. It is a self-enclosed fourteen-line unit with its own integrity, story and moral purpose. Its poetic quality depends upon the employment of a remarkably powerful extended metaphor, not likely to gratify arachnophobes. True, it is written in couplets, but other poems in this collection share that characteristic (39, 75, 76). The passage is taken from a little-known work by Edward FitzGerald (the famous translator-adapter of the *Rubaiyat of Omar Khayyam*), an adaptation of Attar's *Bird Parliament* (lines 894–907). (This rare poem has recently been reissued in the Everyman's Poetry series.)

116 See 99.

119 This sonnet takes the unusual step of dividing itself into two exactly equal halves, with a strong full-stop at the end of line 7 and a clear shift of meaning after that point. The sonnet in general would lose a great deal if it fell frequently into such a simple symmetrical pattern, but the idea of doing this once is most imaginative.

122 This is a sonnet which resists all formal classification in terms of metre or rhyme-scheme, both of which are wildly irregular. The line-lengths run from iambic trimeter, only six syllables (line 11), to full anapaestic tetrameter (line 7) and beyond that in the last line which runs to fifteen syllables. These wide variations make it impossible to systematise the metrical pattern of the poem. The rhyme-scheme, meanwhile, seems reasonable at first sight, beginning with an alternating quatrain *abab* and ending with a straightforward couplet. But chaos prevails in between, leaving one line (12) without a rhyme, unless you are prepared to accept that 'go' rhymes with 'flown' and 'lone'. Even allowing that we are left with this complex scheme: *ababaccdedeeff*. (Disallowing the false rhyme, this would read *ababaccdedefgg*.) All of this is about as irregular as a sonnet could get without falling into twentieth-century formlessness. For all that, this is still a recognisable sonnet.

130 **Castalia**: a fountain of Parnassus (the Classical seat of poetry and music), flowing with waters that inspired the gift of poetry. **Mount Latmos**: the mountain where Endymion pastured his flocks when Selene, goddess of the moon, fell in love with him. **Lethe**: one of the rivers of Hades, causing forgetfulness in all who drank from it.

131 This sonnet is a response to the assassination of Tsar Alexander II on 13 March 1881.

145 The curious rhyming of this sonnet makes one wonder about its purpose. After an orthodox opening with an alternating quatrain *abab*, the fifth line ends in 'dawn'. This has no real rhyme anywhere in the poem. It rhymes with itself as far away as line 11, and perhaps it is meant also to rhyme with the word 'corn'. That is unfortunate because the 'r' in corn debars the rhyme from full legitimacy. Worse than that, however, is the fact that six lines rhyme together with great clumsiness (2 dawn and 4 corn), including all of the last four. This may all be poor technique, but it looks more like a misguided experiment of some sort.

149 and *150* These are two sections from a four-sonnet-length work entitled *Hermaphroditus*, inspired by a famous hermaphrodite statue in the Louvre Museum, Paris, which Swinburne saw in 1863. The story of Hermaphroditus comes from Ovid. A young boy of that name and the nymph, Salacis, are fused together to form a creature of both sexes.

165 A sonnet strictly controlled by rhyme, but allowing much latitude in line-length. Each line has six stressed syllables, but the number of unstressed syllables varies. By contrast, the rhymes are rigidly organised: *abba abba ccd ccd*. There are only four rhymes to the entire sonnet, which is as tight a restriction as will ever be found. This may sound orthodox, but the rhymes themselves are imaginative, producing such unusual pairings as and some/handsome/began some/ransom.

183 This is the celebrated 'sonnet in reverse', in which the 'terminal' couplet precedes the three quatrains.

185 The title recalls the opening line of 97.

187 This sonnet distinguishes itself by some fine approximate rhyming.

189 Petrarch could never have envisioned this extreme development of his product. Nevertheless this is a perfect Italian sonnet: *abbaabba cdcdee*.

Index of Authors

Figures in italic indicate sonnet numbers

List of Titles and First Lines

101 Chaucer (An old man in a lodge within a park)

102 The Cross of Snow (In the long, sleepless watches of the night)

103 The Kraken (Below the thunders of the upper deep)

104 Poets and their Bibliographies (Old poets foster'd under friendlier skies)

105 Buonaparte (He thought to quell the stubborn hearts of oak)

106 A Question by Shelley ('Then what is life?' I cried. From his rent deeps)

107 A Farewell to Poetry (Long hast thou wandered on the happy mountain)

108 The Mute Lovers on the Railway Journey (They bade farewell; but neither spoke of love)

109 Letty's Globe (When Letty had scarce passed her third glad year)

110 On Seeing a Little Child Spin a Coin of Alexander the Great (This is the face of him, whose quick resource)

111 The Quiet Tide Near Ardrossan (On to the beach the quiet waters crept)

112 Silence (There are some qualities – some incorporate things)

113 To my Mother (Because I feel that, in the Heavens above)

114 To Science (Science! True daughter of Old Time thou art!)

115 From *Bird Parliament* (And as the World upon her victims feeds)

116 The Dead (I see them, – crowd on crowd they walk the earth)

117 The Sun God (I saw the Master of the Sun. He stood)

118 Sorrow (Count each affliction, whether light or grave)

119 On Peaceful Death and Painful Life (Why dost thou sorrow for the happy dead?)

120 Brother and Sister (1) (I cannot choose but think upon the time)

121 Brother and Sister (2) (Long years have left their writing on my brow)

122 Misgivings (When ocean-clouds over inland hills)

123 Austerity of Poetry (That son of Italy who tried to blow)

124 East London ('Twas August, and the fierce sun overhead)

125 The Good Shepherd with the Kid (*He saves the sheep, the goats he doth not save*)

126 Quiet Work (One lesson, Nature, let me learn of thee)

127 Shakespeare (Others abide our question. Thou art free)

128 Lucifer in Starlight (On a starred night Prince Lucifer uprose)

129 A Sonnet (A Sonnet is a moment's monument)

130 John Keats (The weltering London ways where children weep)

131 Czar Alexander II (13 March 1881) (From him did forty million serfs, endowed)

132 The Church Porch (Sister, first shake we off the dust we have)

Acknowledgements

The editor and publishers would like to thank the following for permission to reproduce copyright material:

Associated University Presses for George Santayana, 'As in the midst of battle there is room . . .' from *Complete Poems of George Santayana*, Bucknell University Press;

Campbell Thomson & McLaughlin Ltd on behalf of the author for Noel Petty, 'Air-Raid Warning' from *How to be Well-Versed in Poetry*, Penguin Books (1990). Copyright © 1990 Noel Petty;

Peter Fallon Literary Agent on behalf of the Trustees of the Estate of the author for Patrick Kavanagh, 'Lines Written on a Seat on the Grand Canal, Dublin "Erected to the Memory of Mrs Dermot O'Brien" ';

Wolfgang Görtschacher on behalf of the University of Salzburg for Edward Lowbury, 'Vicarious' from *Collected Poems 1934–1992*, University of Salzburg, 1993;

W. W. Norton & Company for E. E. Cummings, 'next to of course god america i' from *Complete Poems 1904–1962*, ed. George J. Firmage. Copyright © 1991 by the Trustees for the E. E. Cummings Trust and George James Firmage;

Oxford University Press for Ivor Gurney, 'On Somme' from *Selected Poems of Ivor Gurney*, ed. P. J. Kavanagh, 1990;

Penguin Books UK and Alfred A. Knopf Inc. for John Updike, 'No More Access to Her Underpants' from *Facing Nature*. Copyright © 1985 by John Updike;

A. P. Watt Ltd on behalf of Michael B. Yeats and Simon and Schuster for W. B. Yeats, 'Leda and the Swan' from *The Poems of W. B. Yeats: A new Edition*, ed. Richard J. Finneran. Copyright © 1928 by Macmillan Publishing Company, renewed 1956 by Georgia Yeats;

Every effort has been made to trace all the copyright holders, but if any have been inadvertently overlooked the publishers will be pleased to make the necessary arrangement at the first opportunity.